Your Towns and Cities in th

Northampton
in the Great War

Your Towns and Cities in the Great War

Northampton
in the Great War

Kevin Turton

Pen & Sword
MILITARY

First published in Great Britain in 2016 by
PEN & SWORD MILITARY
an imprint of
Pen and Sword Books Ltd
47 Church Street
Barnsley
South Yorkshire S70 2AS

Copyright © Kevin Turton, 2016

ISBN 978 1 47383 416 3

Printed and bound in England
by CPI Group (UK) Ltd, Croydon, CR0 4YY

Typeset in Times New Roman by Chic Graphics

Pen & Sword Books Ltd incorporates the imprints of
Pen & Sword Archaeology, Atlas, Aviation, Battleground, Discovery,
Family History, History, Maritime, Military, Naval, Politics, Railways,
Select, Social History, Transport, True Crime, Claymore Press,
Frontline Books, Leo Cooper, Praetorian Press, Remember When,
Seaforth Publishing and Wharncliffe.

For a complete list of Pen and Sword titles please contact
Pen and Sword Books Limited
47 Church Street, Barnsley, South Yorkshire, S70 2AS, England
E-mail: enquiries@pen-and-sword.co.uk
Website: www.pen-and-sword.co.uk

Contents

Acknowledgements

I would like to thank all the writers of the works below, Northampton Central Library, and especially Maureen Yule, whose patience knows no bounds and without whom this book would have been incomplete.

History of the Northamptonshire Regiment
The War to End Wars 1914-1918, Readers Digest
Rotherham at War and Peace, Margaret Drinkall

A Northampton Century, Educational Association
Twentieth Century Pubs, John Wilson
Northampton General Hospital Archives
Victorian Northamptonshire
The *Northampton Mercury* Archive, Central Library
Kelly's Directory 1922, Central Library
Spartacus-Educational.com
Life Went On 1914-1916, Steve Bence and Andrew Dace
The *Evening Telegraph*
The Rugby History Society

Introduction

Comparatively little has been written about Northampton in the Great War of 1914-1918, yet like other towns across the country this was a war that changed forever how people in the town lived, worked and endured. The war placed huge demands on both those who stayed at home and those who enlisted. It changed the way industry operated, broke down barriers and created opportunity, particularly for women. In an age of empire, when all wars were fought in far-off lands with exotic names, 1914 brought war to the Home Front.

Every aspect of life was affected, changed and influenced by this catastrophic conflict once the guns opened fire on the other side of the Channel. Men left their work and put on khaki. The town watched them march off to fight. Homes lost their breadwinners. Industries were forced to change long-held views and working practices. Women found both a place and a voice hitherto denied them, and Ivor Novello wrote, 'Keep the Home Fires Burning', which awakened in the civilian population a sense of patriotism never before seen. This was an immense war, fought on an immense scale that damaged virtually every family in Northampton; such was its impact.

From this distance in time it is extremely difficult to grasp the enormity of the changes wrought upon not only the town but also every individual that lived through it, either at home or in a trench. It has always puzzled me why people allowed the war to continue when they could see the losses. How the commanders of these huge armies succeeded in killing so many men and were left in place to continue the carnage for almost five years. But the more I studied the war and how Northampton reacted to it the more I began to comprehend the mood of those who lived through those years. It was a first. No war of this type had ever been fought before. No one, not even the generals, I would guess, had any real idea of the impact modern warfare would have on the way battles were to be fought. In turn, those left at home had no understanding either of what it meant when their sons, husbands, fathers and daughters enlisted to fight the Hun.

For the first time in history the Home Front, which had spent every other war cossetted and generally untouched by its impact, found itself at the forefront. Women were actively encouraged to recruit men into the armed services, wasteland was ploughed and planted to increase crop yields for food, families dug up their gardens, the army formed Home Guard units, workers were persuaded to buy War Bonds, and in many places Zeppelins successfully crossed the Channel and bombed towns. This was a people's war in all respects and nothing would ever be the same again.

The years 1914 to 1918 challenged the ingenuity and stoicism of a whole community. What I have tried to do in the following narrative is show how the people of Northampton met those challenges, how they reacted to the war, and what exactly happened in the town throughout these years. The way they raised funds, met demands made upon them by the military, handled the huge numbers of wounded, coped with the loss of freedom demanded by the government, and how Northampton's men volunteered in their thousands to leave civilian life and don uniforms, many never returning, and many who did left severely handicapped by their experiences.

This is Northampton's story of the Great War.

CHAPTER 1

1914

A Sense of Excitement

As 1913 was consigned to history and new year celebrations welcomed in 1914, there was the usual hope and expectation by most people that it would be a better, more successful year than its predecessor. There were certainly no thoughts of war. In fact, it's doubtful any country in Europe saw conflict on the horizon. War, due to an everlasting round of shifting alliances, would have been seen by most as simply impossible. Here in Britain there had been no serious involvement in conflict since the Crimea in the 1850s, a long-ago war that made little impact and by this time was a distant memory. So, when people across the county returned to work at the start of January 1914 they were returning to the familiar, perhaps even mundane, routine of life with little expectation of change.

Northampton at this time had a population of around 95,000. Most were centred in or around the town, living in mainly terraced, poor-quality housing, often damp, with poor sanitation, and space at a premium. According to county statistics collated at the end of 1913, of that total 29,700 were men of working age with the main employer being the shoe industry. In fact, approximately 12,000 men and 6,000 women of varying skills depended upon the wages it paid to provide for their families. The rest of the workforce held down jobs in engineering, the various breweries, flour mills or the building industry.

Gold Street, Northampton.

So, overall, it's fair to say the town was deemed relatively prosperous, though not without its problems. Industrial relations, particularly in that footwear sector, had suffered through the latter part of 1913. Sales and manufacturing success during the previous two or three years had also brought with it a number of complex problems, particularly when quality had become paramount and quantity a necessity, which in turn had begun to have a detrimental impact on the leather market causing unexpected shortages. In turn that had pushed up prices and pulled down demand in the industry's traditional market. Footwear with a longer lifespan meant replacement was less frequent. This caused the business owners to seek out new markets away from everyday wear and into the fashionable, more expensive, high end market where customers could afford to pay a higher premium. Inevitably, these changes impacted negatively on the workforce. Lower productivity meant fewer workers needed and, in many cases, fewer hours to be worked. By spring 1914, this combination of market forces and business trends caused most of Northampton's shoe factories to put their workforce on short time. With less money to live on and rents to pay, this led to inevitable disputes and a growing sense of anger, particularly amongst the union representatives who were being pressured by their members to bring the factory owners to the table and effect a change.

The much heralded meeting between the Shoe Manufacturers Association and the National Union of Boot and Shoe Operatives eventually took place in Northampton in May. A long day of discussion followed, with concessions being made by both parties until, eventually, a mutual agreement, far more significant than they could possibly have realised at the time, was finally reached. They agreed to a complete change in working practices: a new minimum wage – essentially an increase of one shilling (5p) from January 1915 and a further one shilling from December 1916; an overtime restriction limiting hours worked to a certain number of weeks in the year; women to be included in the new wage structure with no unauthorised strikes or lock-outs; a restriction on boy labour; and, most important of all, that the growing trend for Northampton's shoe industry to operate in a more high class trade would cease.

Street map of Northampton as it was in 1914.

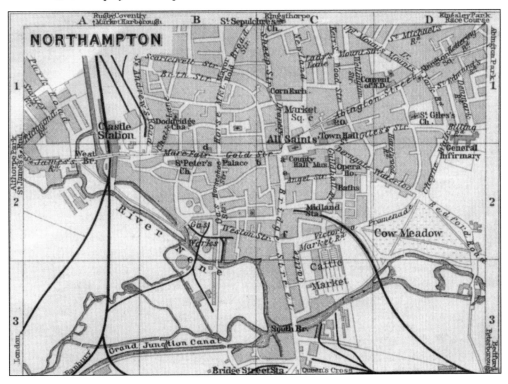

Barratts shoe factory.

They would move back to factories working any and all grades. Heralded as a positive move forward by the *Northampton Mercury*, it set in motion the changes needed by the industry to ensure future growth. Agreement to work in all aspects of shoe and boot manufacture safeguarded its short-term future, but also set it up to be able to handle the mass production that would be required as summer turned to autumn, a factor that would not have been recognised by that May meeting. In fact, it's doubtful that anyone living in Northampton ever fully realised the effect war would have on the town, even when it became inevitable.

When the Black Hand terrorist group assassinated Archduke Franz Ferdinand and his wife Sophie in Sarajevo in June 1914, it made little impact here. Why would it? Assassinating heads of state was not unknown. It had happened in Italy, Portugal, America and France in the past without causing much of a ripple in the world's politics. Besides, it was all a long way from Britain. Certainly it's fair to say that, apart from the actual terrorist attack, there was little reported in the newspapers to cause any alarm. Not even when Austria declared war on Serbia on 28 July, particularly after the *Northampton Mercury* reported that Prime Minister Asquith had addressed the Commons to ease fears:

Prime Minister Asquith.

> *The House meets under conditions of gravity almost unparalleled. Issues of peace and war are hanging in the balance. It is of vital importance that Britain, who has no interest directly at stake, should present a united front and act with the authority of a united nation.*

From that statement it would have been reasonable for people to assume, as was probably intended, that whatever was taking place all those miles away, would have no immediate impact upon the country. As workers read the prime minister's proclamation over breakfast, it would probably have been dismissed as unimportant – dismissed, discarded and duly ignored. The same newspaper report also pointed out that the strength of the Austrian Army that had embarked upon this war was in the region of half a million men. This was no skirmish then. When, on 31 July, the *Northampton Mercury* reported that Russia, to protect its own interests, had issued a declaration of war in support of Serbia against Austria and that Germany, in response to all this sabre rattling had begun the process of mobilisation, Asquith's notion of neutrality was beginning to look flawed.

From that point on things moved at an alarming speed. The finance markets reacted badly to the threat of war causing the bank rate to shoot up to eight per cent. The London Stock Exchange closed. All German yachts were withdrawn from Cowes Regatta, and overnight food prices shot up. On 1 August, Germany declared war on Russia; two days later they also declared war on France. Britain had signed up as a guarantor of Belgium neutrality under the Treaty of London 1839. The moment German boots touched Belgian soil, Britain was honour-bound to support the alliance. On 4 August, the inevitable happened. Parliament declared war and the country began to mobilise. It was universally agreed that the decision was just. Northampton, like other towns across the country, readily embraced the pronouncement from Asquith, believing that the war would never last but would be a great adventure.

Life would never be the same again.

But in that summer of 1914, despite the clamour for war, nothing was allowed to cancel or reshape the well-established events that had always dominated the summer months in Northampton. At Castle Ashby, the 32nd annual flower show went ahead as planned, drawing huge crowds from the town, many travelling by train to the Marquis of Northampton's open gardens. There, on a hot August day, they watched keenly as a panel of horticultural experts gave their verdicts in the judging of over 1,260 entries in a variety of gardening categories from buttonholes to bouquets, table decorations to window box displays, and miniature model gardens. In Northampton itself the Northampton Hospital held its annual August parade headed by the Brixworth Brass Band, marching through streets lined with supporters and well-wishers as it made its way into Market Square.

Territorial Headquarters on Clare Street.

While all this was happening, with war now certain, notices were being posted all across town and county calling-up all men of the reserve and territorial army, though it was reported later that most men in either service, all too aware of the army's need, had already begun to don uniforms. The notices simply reinforced what they had already guessed. At 9am on 5 August, they marched into town and began to assemble at the Territorial headquarters on Clare Street.

At around the same time, enlisted men of the Northamptonshire Regiment, training at Ashridge Park, Hertfordshire, were ordered back to Northampton. They arrived by train at three o'clock that afternoon to be met by huge, cheering crowds outside the station and all along their route to headquarters. By evening it was also announced that Lord Kitchener had been appointed as secretary of state for war, a man much respected by the general public having fought in a number of colonial wars, though in hindsight not necessarily a man with any real grasp of modern warfare.

Lord Kitchener of Khartoum.

On the food front, impending war brought housewives onto the high street as the summer progressed and shops were suddenly struggling to cope with demand. In turn, that pushed up prices on staple foods like bacon, cheese, butter and sugar. For many, no matter where it was going to be fought, war simply meant shortages on the Home Front. So most sought to stock up as fast as possible. The commonly held view that the conflict would be short-lived, whilst widely believed, held little sway when it came to feeding the family. Neither did the argument put forward by the local business community that the only shortages would be those caused by panic buying, at least in the early stages. But as the government stepped in to allay fears and let it be known that food stocks were high, imports unaffected, and no crisis on the food front anticipated, life once more returned to normal. Prices slowly returned to their pre-war levels and the initial panic subsided.

On 8 August, Parliament passed a key piece of legislation, the Defence of the Realm Act (DORA for short). It was intended to strengthen and enhance the government's hold on power, by creating new laws to control the spread of information throughout the war, and remove some freedoms that it deemed useful to the enemy. In essence it gave sweeping new powers to the police, made spying in all its guises a capital offence, and censored newspapers' reportage and press speculation about the conduct and direction of the war. It would affect every walk of life; though it is doubtful that its full implications were realised at the time. No one was likely to have read the small print, but apart from these key points on a domestic front it also meant that it was illegal to buy binoculars, fly kites, light bonfires or feed bread to wild animals. It also changed the way the licensing trade operated. Pubs had to water down their beer and could only open between 12 to 3pm and 6.30 to 9.30pm, temperance being recommended. Furthermore, and perhaps more importantly, it allowed government to seize land or businesses for any purpose in furtherance of the war effort. That included being able to convert factories, particularly those engaged in engineering, towards the production of munitions for the army. At around the same time they also created the Aliens Restriction Act, which meant foreign nationals resident in the town had to report to local police. Up and down the country, within days of war being declared, demonstrations and occasional riots had already sprung up outside businesses displaying German names or ownership. Rights of citizenship held little sway for some. In Northampton the new law had a devastating effect on one particular individual.

Joseph Gottschalk had moved from Germany to Northampton when he was 18 years old. He had established his home in the town, built a career working for the Municipal Tramways Company, and just before

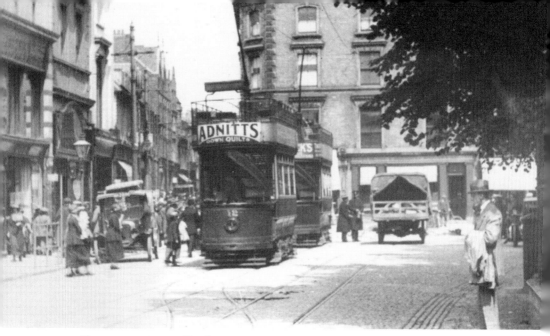

Trams operating in Northampton.

the outbreak of the war had become its manager. He had given up his German nationality in the mid 1890s and probably married his wife, a British woman, at around the same time. Between them they had a son serving in the British Army at the start of the conflict. Joseph was much respected by all who knew him and with some high ranking friends on the council. But the declaration of war changed everything in his life. People he had known and many he had not but had served well turned against him. His German birth, it seems, caused him to become an alien overnight. Public opinion grew ever more hostile. Despite this, Northampton council supported his position heading up the Tramways Company, as did many of the employees; and, realising the implications of the new legislation, held a vote amongst council members to ascertain whether or not they would support him continuing in his role. They voted overwhelmingly in his favour. But Joseph, in the face of so much public opposition, decided he could not accept their support and resigned:

> *In closing my management of the Northampton Corporation Tramways, I desire to express to you my most sincere thanks for the kindness and appreciation I have received from you at all times. I am proud to think that the*

tramways under my management have been extremely
successful, thanks in a large measure to the great help I
have received from an efficient and loyal staff. I deeply
deplore the circumstances which necessitate my leaving
the work I have always loved and I can only conclude with
the earnest hope that the undertaking will continue to
prosper.

One can only sympathise. Certainly the Tramways Company did, as
did Northampton council, who paid him by way of compensation, it is
believed, £300. Others, particularly business owners with German
names found themselves under similar pressure. Some were verbally
abused, others had their premises attacked. For many, Germany was
the aggressor, the warmonger, the cause of the conflict spreading itself
across much of Europe, any links with it or its people simply
unacceptable. Whilst some deplored the new legislation, others
welcomed it. For many of German descent living in Northampton or
around the county, there can be no doubt it was devastating, with many
eventually being interned at Eastcote House, which later also became
a prisoner-of-war camp. At this early stage it was certainly going to be
a difficult war for some groups of people.

The shoe industry, though, saw a sudden increase in business. The
army needed boots. The three companies in Northampton to be
awarded initial contracts for the military were Sears & Co, S. Collier
& Sons, and Crick & Co. For them business was on the up and, as the
war progressed, orders would be spread across footwear companies
throughout the town and across the county. Throughout August and
September 1914, other industries and institutions began to change.

Mulliners, originally carriage-makers based on Bridge Street, had
been making automobile bodies since 1907. Its owner, Arthur Mulliner,
was one of the founder members of the RAC. Their works were
converted to facilitate the manufacture of both munitions and military
vehicles. Northampton Asylum, on Abington Avenue, and Barry Road
School became military hospitals. But what occupied people's thoughts
the most was the army – what it was doing, when would it be involved
in the fighting, whether it could cope with the demands of a European
war, and what was likely to happen about recruitment.

Men queuing to enlist despite the weather.

The government made it clear through a number of reported speeches in the Commons that there would be no need for conscription. The belief still prevailed at the end of the summer that this would not be a long war, though it does appear that Kitchener did not necessarily share that view. Nevertheless, recruitment was vital. Britain in 1914 had a standing army of around 120,000. Compared to the European armies it was hugely inadequate.

Kitchener's volunteer army needed another 100,000 men. So posters began to appear, calling on men to volunteer, and as war fever gripped the town they did. By the end of August, 180 men had joined the ranks, by 3 September that figure had jumped to 358. Meetings were held across town calling on more men to enlist, to do their duty and serve. It's fair to say there was a general feeling across both town

Newly enlisted men still in civvies.

and shire that this was a just war. A war that could be quickly won and one that every man between the ages of 18 and 35 ought to be involved in. By the end of August, with recruitment running at high levels, the first white feathers began to appear.

The white feather was a symbol of cowardice, usually given by a woman to a man, either face to face in the street or posted on anonymously. It was started by retired admiral Charles Penrose Fitzgerald, who had formed the Order of the White Feather in Folkestone, which was a garrison town, to force men to do what he believed to be their duty – join up and fight. With no conscription, and totally dependent on volunteers, he no doubt saw it as his own duty to force men to enlist by fair means or foul by attacking their manhood and sense of honour. He wasn't alone in this thought either. Many of the suffragettes that had been fighting for women's rights adopted a similar stance after agreeing to stop their activities in pursuit of women's right to vote, deciding instead to direct their efforts into supporting the war effort and the need to recruit. The handing out of white feathers was not a method they ever adopted. Instead they used a public platform, organising speeches across the UK to drive home the message that fighting Germany was crucial to the country's survival. They and the admiral were also aided in this aim by Baroness Orczy, author of *The Scarlet Pimpernel*, who formed her Women of England's Active Service League that had very quickly attracted 20,000 members, most of whom signed a pledge:

> *At this hour of England's grave peril and desperate need.*
> *I do hereby pledge myself most solemnly in the name of*
> *my king and country to persuade every man I know to offer*
> *his services to the country, and I also pledge myself never*
> *to be seen in public with any man who, being in every way*
> *fit and free for service, has refused to respond to his*
> *country's call.*

Not that being in receipt of one of these feathers was ever generally openly reported, but the practice was well-known. National newspapers carried the stories from across the country and, in town and throughout the outlying districts, the practice of handing out feathers had become

BY FRANK HARDWICK.

THE COBBLER: Find room to put you up? Certainly, my lad. We'll do what we can for you now, and p'raps you will do what you can for us soon—eh?

Billeting as illustrated by the Northampton Mercury.

a feature of the early stages of the war. So much so that there was a public call for this to stop on the basis that not every young man was needed for the army, particularly in the countryside where they were needed for agriculture; though even that would change with time.

On 28 August, it was announced through the local press that all public buildings and licensed houses were to be used by the army as billets for soldiers, and that if more were needed they would begin to use private houses. This was to accommodate the influx of Welsh soldiers who were to be brought to Northampton for training before being sent on to France. Sixteen thousand men of the Royal Welsh Fusiliers began arriving on 3 September, ferried north from Wales on fifty-four trains throughout the day. They were met outside the station by vociferous crowds waving flags and cheering them on as they marched in column towards town. Over the following four months they became a constant presence as they were paraded through the streets along with their artillery, generally on route to the racecourse, which they shared at times with the new recruits and where they carried out various manoeuvres and exercises in front of a watching crowd of enthusiasts. At around the same time the cattle market was taken over for the stabling of horses. Farriers and foragers moved in to maintain the health and well-being of the various horses used by the Welsh Division but particularly the heavy horses used by the artillery. Elsewhere, Abington Park became home for the 5th Cheshires. Northampton had changed in the space of a few weeks into a town on a war footing.

For some Northampton families the war seemed even nearer. The 1st Battalion Northampton Regiment had already been sent to France, landing at Le Havre on 13 August. They were part of the British Expeditionary Forces (BEF) that had been sent across the Channel to link up with the French army. After the fall of Liege in early August, these families knew there was going to be a battle of some sort and that the Northamptonshire Regiment was likely to be involved. They were keen to hear news, but such news was difficult to obtain. Like families before and since they were worried. They wanted to know what was happening; and for those families whose sons had enlisted they probably wanted reassurance. For many, that came on 28 August when

The Royal Welsh Fusiliers along with their mascot.

the *Northampton Mercury* published a letter from the front from an unnamed officer in the regiment:

> There's a cheery, confident swing about us, a fearless determined air, though each one realises that maybe the long moving line will be shorter when it returns and, maybe it will never come back again. Every man goes to fight perfectly equipped. Take our own case, and it is typical. I have before me a list of 45 different articles of clothing and appurtenances which have been given to us. They range from both toothbrush to greatcoat, from bible to cardigan waistcoat. They have given us needles and cotton, woollen wraps, two pairs of boots each, hair brushes, shirts, socks, and many other things. If we suffer hardships it will be no fault of our equipment.
>
> We carry haversacks. Inside them there fits a waterproof case, now filled with two tins of bully beef and eight biscuits – two days rations. We have large service revolvers and a lot of ammunition, map carriers, compasses, field glasses, water bottles, mess tins, and

other accessories. The organisation up to this stage has proved wonderful.

There is little more to say. We are coming back if we possibly can, because we want to live. But if honour demands that we should not, we'll face our fate, every mother's son of us.

Probably as good a recruitment poster as you could get. Perhaps that's why the newspaper published it. Things at the front were obviously fine. Of course we now know that would change. But to people living in Northampton in 1914, it was important to feel confident that the war was going well.

Edgar Mobbs on a rare visit home from the Front.

At about the same time news broke about one of Northampton's sporting heroes, Northampton Saints and England international rugby player, Edgar Mobbs. At the age of 32 he had been refused an officer commission at the outbreak of war because the army deemed him too old. But Mobbs was not so easily put off. Enlisting as a private soldier he decided that his name alone ought to carry weight amongst other sportsmen, so much so that he could become a catalyst that brought them into the army to serve together. On 3 September at the Plough Hotel in Northampton, he organised a meeting of past and present rugby players with the sole intention of forming a local corps for Kitchener's army. The target was to bring together 300 men, many of whom would know each other, and keep them together as part of the Northamptonshire regiment:

> It was a time when every man between the ages of nineteen
> and thirty-five should come to the assistance of the Empire.

The Plough Hotel as it looks today.

The target was easily exceeded, such was the esteem in which he was held. Mobbs went on to use his influence within the rugby fraternity to organise matches between the services and professional teams, all the time calling for men to enlist, using his name and profile to persuade others to join the ranks and fight a war he obviously believed to be just. 'Mobbs Own', as it became known, continued to grow in number as more and more men rallied to his call, eventually forming the backbone of the 7th Battalion Northamptonshire Regiment and in time gaining him the commission the army had originally denied him.

While all this was happening, another famous Northampton sportsman joined the army, almost unnoticed and with a different regiment. Walter Tull, a professional footballer who had been sold by Tottenham Hotspur to the Cobblers (Northampton FC) in 1911, was the grandson of a slave, brought up for much of his childhood in an orphanage, and an exceptionally gifted footballer. According to the club's history he had played 111 times as a forward for Northampton. Held in high regard in the football world, he joined what was known as the Footballers' Battalion (Middlesex Regiment) along with his brother. Like Mobbs, he was highly respected by all who knew him, and also like Mobbs, eventually achieved an officer commission.

Throughout August and into September the rush to enlist overwhelmed the recruiting office in Northampton and, in order to process men more quickly, a call went out for more doctors. It was vital, of course, to assess fitness levels before they were allowed to enlist. Not all volunteers were accepted at this stage of the war. In 1914, standards were rigorous. They would be relaxed as the war progressed, but for those who queued to sign their name in the early stages, rules were strictly adhered to.

Reasons for volunteering, of course, were varied. For many it was simple patriotism. The country had a war to fight and it was up to every man to do his duty. Certainly, that was the message constantly pushed out, whether via posters, local council meetings, Sunday morning worship or the local press. Britain at this time had an empire. Supporting it, protecting it and fighting for it was a part of every child's education and a generation had grown up with a tacit understanding of just what the words 'empire' and 'duty' meant and stood for.

Some volunteered because their lives were hard. A fair number of families existed on or below the breadline. Joining the services meant a regular wage, maybe even regular meals and an escape perhaps from the daily grind of life, away from shifts, low wages, short-time working or, for some, unemployment. Others volunteered because their friends or workmates were joining. Being the odd one out was no place to be if you wanted the respect of those around you. Peer pressure is always difficult to ignore.

There was also the element of adventure war brings. In the early stages of the conflict there was clearly a view that it was an opportunity, no matter how fleeting, to escape the mundane, do something outside the normal routines of life that otherwise would be unattainable. Because, as was believed at the time by most, it would all be over by Christmas. For these men altruism played no part. All these factors combined had, by the end of September 1914, caused 4,500 men from the county to join. But Kitchener decided he wanted more. The figure needed by the army had now risen to 1 million men. The first battles, Mons and the Marne, had already been fought and casualties were high. The first figures published in Northampton were for the retreat from Mons earlier that month. For local people it was the first time they would get a sense of the losses to come:

	Officers	Other ranks
Killed	36	127
Wounded	57	629
Missing	<u>95</u>	<u>4,183</u>
	188	4,939

As they looked at the numbers they were also able to read the names of those of the Northamptonshire Regiment that formed part of the statistics. No doubt it made sober reading, as did reports of the sudden influx of Belgian refugees.

After the fall of Liege and the German advance, thousands across Belgium were displaced, many seeking shelter in Britain. The first numbers that arrived in Northamptonshire were housed in Kettering.

Belgian refugees on the road after the German invasion.

Then, as numbers grew, there were refugees housed in Wellingborough, Oundle, Northampton and a number of outlying villages. In early October the Mayor of Northampton, Councillor G. W. Beattie, launched the Belgian Relief Fund, and in an impassioned plea to the people of Northampton asked them to donate money to help with their upkeep. Local support was never in doubt, the response was huge with £500 raised within days. To help lift the profile of the refugees and bring their plight to more people across the county, the mayoress organised what was to be called The Belgian Rose Day. Set for 24 October, it was to be run by the ladies of the town. The Belgian flag would be flown over the council offices, buttonholes fashioned in the Belgian colours and sold for one penny each along with pennants and small flags, all proceeds going to the fund. It was a huge success. By the time of the celebration day, thirty children had arrived from Belgium and been housed all along the Kettering Road, and more were already on route. The consequences of war were clearly evident, people gave generously, and the fund quickly rose to over £1,900.

As October 1914 drew to a close, the town started to see its first casualties, who were initially all Belgian soldiers. They began arriving

Northampton General Hospital 1914-1918.

in the last week of the month with most taken to Cottesbrooke Hall, whose relatively new owner, Captain Robert Brassey, had converted it in part to take soldiers in need of convalescence. They were quickly followed by British wounded brought by train into Northampton where, on arrival, they were assessed as to the nature of their wounds then split up according to their needs, some sent out to Weston Favell, some to Kettering, but most taken to Northampton General Hospital.

The St John's Ambulance Brigade held a meeting on King Street to inform its members that it would need to set up a temporary hospital as more casualties were expected to arrive over the coming weeks, but they desperately needed furniture and equipment of all types. An appeal was launched to the people of Northampton to help provide as much as they could. The response was overwhelming.

Belgian Day was allocated 31 October, as a follow-up to the Rose Day that had been held a week earlier. The town was in need of more funds to aid the influx of Belgian refugees who had continued to arrive. The ladies who had organised the first event set about organising the second. Perhaps having learned from the initial experience, this time they organised a variety of different ways of obtaining money from the general public. They continued to sell buttonholes, flags and flowers in the Belgian colours but this time, in order to maximise sales, they boarded buses, trains, stopped workers as they left for home, canvassed door-to-door, stood along Wellingborough Road stopping passers-by, and brought in the scouts. They then organised parades, brass bands, torchlight processions and street entertainers. It was a huge success. People embraced the charity and understood the need. Many agreed to pay a weekly subscription of a few pennies every week and the refugee fund was secure.

While all this was going on, the churches across town and county were asked to raise funds specifically for Northampton General Hospital. The need for nursing care and all that implies had grown significantly over the previous two months and there was a growing feeling that those same services would be in ever-increasing demand. Money was in short supply. The churches launched their own appeals and by the end of the first week in November had raised £500.

On 10 November, at a meeting held at Northampton Town Hall and chaired by the lord mayor, it was agreed to form a citizens' corps. People had been clamouring for weeks for something to be done about local defence. Not that there was fear of invasion. It was more to do with organising those too old to fight or those rejected on health

Cartoons used to embarrass those who had not joined the colours.

THE LAST OF THE NUTS OF SANDY COVE,
(Or how to make use of our stay-at-homes.)

Lady in the Background (also engaged in making nightwear for the wounded): I say! I wonder if you would be so good as to lend him to us when you have finished with him.

grounds, and giving them a role. In fact, by the time the mayor had stood up to speak, 300 men had already put their names down to join. It was widely publicised that Lord Kitchener was strongly in favour, which obviously gave credence to the idea. The Territorials had also given permission for their headquarters on Clare Street to be used in the evenings and on a Sunday, though they did add the proviso that forty hours drill must be put in by every volunteer before they could be considered worthy of joining the new corps. As an incentive, they would also issue proficiency certificates to every man who completed these drill requirements. The drills, insisted the Territorials, must also include rifle practice. This gave rise to an immediate issue. These had to be purchased at 28 shillings each (£1.40). But the meeting agreed that, collectively, they would meet the cost. The corps was formed and by the end of that month it had 1,200 men in its ranks.

At around the same time as recruitment began to waiver, a little census of sorts was carried around the local villages to try and ascertain whether or not the call to arms was being met everywhere. The results confirmed that the response had been huge. Below are the figures published at the time:

	Enlisted
Great and Little Billing	18
Castle Ashby	20
Church and Chapel Brampton	30
Cogenhoe	10
Creaton	17
Harpole	24
Kilsby	27
Lamport, Hanging Houghton, Faxton	15
Long Buckby	141
Moulton	23
Scaldwell	27
Wootton	30
Yardley Hastings	28

Alongside these numbers it was also recorded that in some of the villages the whole male population had joined the army, but without exception no men of serving age were left behind. The call to be a part of this war had not gone unheeded, and these were only a small number of the villages that made up the county.

Throughout November, news filtered through about a huge battle taking place at Ypres. The weekly casualty lists were reflecting an ever-increasing loss of life. Photographs of those killed filled the pages of the *Northampton Mercury*, many from the Northamptonshire Regiment. If people had any doubts as to what was happening on the Western Front the newspaper began to publish letters from the wounded. One such letter from a Sergeant Fletcher, writing home to his father-in-law in Northampton, gives a vivid account of the fighting he had been involved in through the autumn and just how bad it was out there:

> *We commenced to drive the Germans out of France, and then the fun started. We followed the Germans toward the river Aisne, where the great battle was fought, but we had three small fights before we got there, and in one of these we lost captain Hewat ... in these small fights we lost about 300 men. At the Aisne my battalion was ordered to cross the bridge on Sunday morning September 13. German shells were flying all around us, but strange to say we lost only one killed and one wounded. The next day we got pepper. We had advanced up a hill at four in the morning. It was raining in torrents. We got to within 150 yards of the enemy, so close in fact that our own artillery shells were bursting amongst us. Then by some means the Germans got on our flank with a machine gun. We had to retire into a wood and there I received a bayonet wound in the back of my leg. I had to lie down and bandage myself, and by the time I had finished I was surrounded. I had to sit without food for two days and two nights in the wood for fear of being captured. I got away eventually and re-joined my regiment, only to find I was the only NCO left in my company. The fight I have described was where we lost brave captain Price. He had the side of his face blown off while he was cheering on his men. In the big battle*

which followed we lost nearly all our officers and about 300 men ... After some hard marching we reached Ypres in snow and rain on November 15 ... We were standing in about a foot of mud when a shell burst over us ... then another shell came. I saw a flash in front of me, and I went down with a piece of shrapnel in my left thigh.

It is surprising that under the censorship laws in place at the time an account so graphic was able to be sent on to a family and eventually published. How people reacted when they read this is impossible to know, but it probably began to change views, particularly in light of the fact that Kitchener had made it clear by this time that he would need an army that was more than double the size of that he had originally envisaged. For the town this news from the Front was compounded by further bad news from the navy. HMS *The Good Hope*, flagship of Rear Admiral Sir Christopher Craddock, had been sunk in the Battle of Coronel off the Chilean coast, killing all 919 officers and men, some of whom came from Northampton. November proved to be an exceptionally bad month for the town and county.

The exception was those in the shoe and boot industry. Their wages had increased, with many now earning around £3 a week. Back in September 1914, when it had started to receive its share of government contracts, it had begun to ramp-up productivity with the needs of the military being paramount. Those domestic markets, which had been in decline throughout the first half of the year, were to some extent ignored. But as demand increased so did the labour problems. Understandably, a number of the overall workforce had left the industry to take up arms, so a restructuring of sorts was required to maintain full production. Women eventually became a key factor in this overall planning and by late December Northampton's shoe factories were at full capacity again, producing boots for both the British and French armies, with contracts being awarded that would keep production schedules running until the end of February 1915, and more work was obviously in the offing. The average life-span of footwear in the trenches was only six weeks, so continuity of work was not in doubt. The downside of this sudden increase in demand was that the cost of

The departure of the Welsh Fusiliers from Northampton in December 1914. (Northampton Central Library)

leather used to produce boots for the military had begun to rise with each passing month. As Christmas arrived, it had risen by twenty-five per cent and the type of leather used in the manufacture of soles and the underside of these boots had risen by as much as 100 per cent of its mid-summer price. Signs were that these prices would continue to rise if imports could not be maintained. But, in December 1914, that was a problem for another year.

As was the billeting of soldiers. The Welsh Fusiliers, the 16,000 men that had been so warmly welcomed into Northampton three months earlier, had been billeted across town. December saw them finally leave to face an uncertain future and, with much pomp, they marched to the sound of brass bands, through flag waving crowds towards the railway station, where they were eventually carried off toward the Front. For many people it was a sad moment. Not just because they were going off to fight, and by now people had begun to understand just what that meant, but because, in many cases, they had become friends. The town had grown used to their presence, watched them on manoeuvres on the racecourse, met them in pubs, joined them at social events, heard them sing at various musical concerts, and generally grown used to having them around. As they waved them off on the convoy of trains that took them south, there was genuine regret.

But despite all that and the constant tragedy of the weekly casualty lists, Christmas was celebrated as usual as possible. The cinemas, a constant source of information about the war through newsreels, were showing *The Call*, starring Clara Kimbell-Young (a hugely popular American film star), and Charles Dickens' *A Christmas Carol*, while the Northampton Opera House, in aid of the Red Cross Fund and the Good Samaritan Society, brought in a new play by Irene Osgood, *The Menace*. American by birth, she had spent most of her life in Britain and was well-known as both a novelist and a playright. This was a bit of a coup for Northampton, particularly as the play itself was topical, telling the story of the fictional Baron Von Stoll, a German spy who, in his disguise as a financier, befriends an aristocratic widow and her daughter. A convoluted plot sees him use the family to gain access to military information that he

Advert that ran in the Northampton Mercury *advertising the Christmas play.*

can send back to Germany to facilitate an invasion of Britain. But, of course, he is eventually unmasked, much to the delight of the audiences that packed the theatre on six consecutive nights.

For those fighting at the Front, various funds were raised both in Northampton and across the shire, which had been used to buy things for the troops. These items were then sent across the Channel for distribution amongst the men. Alongside these were the Princess Mary gift boxes. Advertisements ran in both the national and the local press asking for monetary contributions to a sailors' and soldiers' Christmas fund, and Northampton, along with other towns, gave generously. The money bought a small brass box that usually contained cigarettes, tobacco, a lighter, maybe a pipe and a greetings card. By Christmas Day, 355,000 had been distributed amongst the troops, in the hope, no doubt, that Christmas would be celebrated despite the hardships, and that perhaps 1915 would be a better year.

CHAPTER 2

1915
In the Grip of War

The new year dawned with stalemate on the Western Front, with neither side winning and neither side moving forward. All movement had effectively stopped. The armies on all sides had effectively fought themselves to a standstill. Trench warfare was to become the order of the day. Elsewhere, Turkey had entered the war on Germany's side at the end of 1914, partly due to its fear of Russia and what it saw as Russia's designs upon the Dardanelles, a part of the world relatively unknown to most but a place that would soon become known to all. So, the war had not ended at Christmas but had become, as the poet Siegfried Sassoon later wrote, 'mainly a matter of holes and ditches'.

Back home the weather had been atrocious. The first half of January saw nothing but rain, which caused widespread flooding across the whole county. Many roads outside town were impassable and life for many at best difficult, for farmers simply miserable. Added to this early gloom was the fact that the cost of living, according to government, had risen by twenty per cent. The cost of meat had been driven up by the demand to feed both the British and French military. Sugar, bacon and cheese had also climbed in price. Were it not for imports of beef at favourable prices from Ireland, the cost of a Sunday roast would have hit an all-time high. As it was, families were finding money tight. Only the successes of the Royal Navy in keeping shipping routes open had

ZEPPELIN RAIDS.

ALL PERSONS liable to be called out for Raid Duty should carry a

Luminous Watch

These Watches are obtainable

at 5/6 each,

FROM

W. Horden & Son

29, HIGH STREET, KETTERING.

Advertisers were quick to use the notion of Zeppelin attacks in their advertising.

managed to keep the cost of grain down, which obviously affected a number of foodstuffs, including flour for bread. They ensured that merchant ships from Argentina and America continued to arrive at British ports unhindered, though even that had its problems. An indirect consequence of this action meant fish were being landed in ever-decreasing quantities because trawlers were being used in minesweeping operations that helped keep those crucial sea lanes open. At the Town Hall the mayor was trying hard to defend his policy of dimming or, in places, turning off the street lights. Zeppelins had already made their presence felt on the Continent. The Belgian refugees had been able to testify to that. There was a real fear that, should they manage to travel this far inland, they would wreak havoc. Having streets lit was, according to the prevalent political view, akin to lighting their way from coast to town. Flying with little navigational aids meant they were totally dependent upon what they could see and hear, so any form of light, church bells and audible clocks were a key direction and target locator.

But the mayor's view of possible attack had its fair share of critics and certainly not all agreed that his measures to counteract any possible air-raid had merit. At various meetings in Northampton, it led to some vicious arguments in opposition by those who felt that these

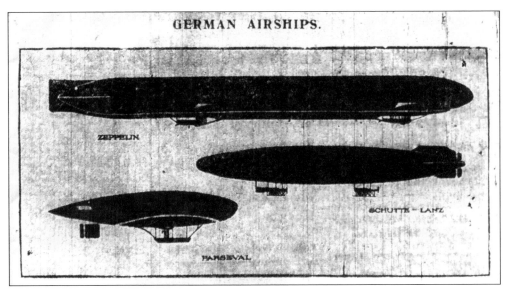

GERMAN AIRSHIPS.

ZEPPELIN

SCHUTTE - LANZ

PARSEVAL

Images of Zeppelins intended to make the public aware.

precautions added an extra burden to those at home and hurt trade. People less likely to be out shopping on a winter's night when they couldn't find their way home in the dark was the most vociferous argument mounted by the retail and licensing trade, though this was not supported by the police or the public at large, most of whom were in accord with the mayor. Despite the argument put forward by some of his council colleagues that the townspeople of Northampton were not afraid of German raiders in the sky, he disagreed, quite rightly, and the policy stayed in place. As the mayor told his critics at a Town Hall meeting, stoicism was all well and good but not when it could cost lives:

> *If the dimming of the lights in the event of a raid meant the saving of but one baby's life in Northampton I would think the step well justified.*

Clearly, some sectors of the town had no idea of the destructive nature of indiscriminate bombing from the air.

So things on the Home Front were not so rosy at the start of 1915, but they were far worse for the Belgian refugees that continued to arrive. These people had lost everything and the town continued in its support to help, despite the difficulties. In fact all across the county, villages were either setting up or operating support funds. Brixworth held a concert to raise money, Irthlingborough agreed to accept more refugees and organised a street parade to raise funds, as did Blisworth, which had its own Belgian Refugee Committee. Other funds came from Wellingborough, Kettering, Thrapston and countless others. There was a determination by all that the families arriving would be supported and funded. It was much needed as more arrived through January. Across the shire committees sprang up to organise not only funds for the refugees but also for a variety of other worthwhile causes. In the main these committees were often chaired or operated and managed by the ladies of the town.

Britain at this time, of course, was very much a class-based culture. Women from the upper strata of Northampton's society were readily accepted as being the most appropriate to manage some of these roles and, therefore, raise the profile of the fund amongst those best placed to support it financially. At the outbreak of the war the Honourable

Women had already been accepted into the Royal Mail.

Evelina Haverfield, an influential suffragette, along with Decima Moore had formed the Women's Volunteer Reserve. Made up of wealthy women, they formed one of the first organisations co-ordinated and operated solely by women, though not cheap to join. Everyone in the WVR had to buy a uniform for £2, so those in the lower earning classes tended to shy away. Nevertheless, it helped pave the way for all women to begin to see that they too had a role. As those less wealthy saw what these women were doing they also began to demand a greater involvement. They began to form themselves into a variety of different types of organisations – the Women's Legion, which became the largest entirely voluntary body; the Women's Auxiliary Force, again voluntary for those wanting to work part-time in canteens or hospitals; the Women's Forage Corp, formed by the government to help source

Woman working in munitions.

forage for the horses involved in the military, and these organisations continued to grow.

As the war progressed, women became ever more involved across all industries, moved away from the volunteer organisations and began taking paid, full-time work, though that did take a little time to achieve. There were some key obstacles to overcome first, and these were clearly demonstrated in Northampton when farmers organised a meeting with the town council and managers of the labour exchange.

In dire need of agricultural workers for the land caused by the country's drive to recruit men into the army, which had severely affected their own workforces, farmers found themselves with a depleted labour force and unable to increase productivity at a time when it was most needed. But they collectively refused to employ women, feeling them unsuited to life on the land. Instead they wanted an agreement that boys aged 12 would be allowed to leave school, be recruited through the labour exchange for farm work, and paid a low wage set by themselves.

Applying the finishing touches

It appears there were no dissenting voices. Northampton County Council readily agreed, but did request that farmers examine the possible role women could play in future should the war continue. There was already a view that women were likely to become indispensable to the war effort and, as time passed, would become an integral part of the labour force. By December 1915, Northampton's women were driving trams, delivering post, making munitions, taking on more skilled work in the boot and shoe industry, and more and more roles once the preserve of men.

Women motorcycle outriders

The government had begun to realise from a relatively early stage that without women's involvement in industry, recruitment for the army would stall. Losses on the Western Front had, by this time, already impacted upon the army's strength, which meant that this situation could not be allowed to develop further. The volunteer army, it seemed, had a voracious appetite and replenishment would become constant. To that end, the army sought out various ways of bringing men to the colours. In Northampton, apart from the posters, advertising and general patriotic fervour still gripped the town, so the Northamptonshire Regiment (known locally as the Steelbacks) organised a recruiting march during the last week of April. A company of 140 men under the command of Colonel Willoughby set out to march their way from Peterborough to Northampton. Their task was to stop off at various places on route, hold meetings, and recruit soldiers. The march was to take a week to complete, include as many outlying villages as possible, address any gathered crowd with the need and virtues of serving in the army, and generally enlist new recruits.

It proved a huge success. Local newspapers followed their progress, huge crowds assembled at every stopover point, and brass bands, cream teas, and a variety of local dignitaries welcomed their arrival every evening. Destinations covered included Oundle, Wadenhoe, Stoke Doyle, Thrapston, Rushden, Irthlingborough, Wellingborough, Northampton and countless hamlets and villages in between. At each day's final destination, the colonel gave a familiar address to the assembled audiences:

> *I strongly urge young ladies not to be seen walking out with young men who are shirking their duty and refusing to do their share in protecting them in this country. After the war any eligible young man who did not take his share in protecting these shores would be looked upon as a shirker, and would be shunned by society. Old as I am I would rather myself take a position in the fighting line than be a shirker myself.*

The march was considered a success with men enlisting at almost every stop over with the total number of new recruits at the end of their marching week reported as being 120. Obviously, that number grew as more men rallied to the flag over the following days and weeks.

The mayor, Councillor Parker, and his wife. (Northampton Mercury)

While all this was ongoing, Northampton's recruitment committee held a meeting in the Town Hall. Organised by the newly elected mayor, Councillor Parker, and three members of parliament, Lord Hugh Cecil, Sir Ryland Adkins and Labour MP Jack Hodge, all of whom shared the stage with a number of prominent local men, including the man many had come to listen to, Edgar Mobbs. It was a patriotic event: the hall was full to the rafters with a sympathetic audience, all of whom had turned out to listen to the argument for war, most of which they had probably heard many times before. But they were there to be persuaded as to its merits, something Lord Hugh did as he opened the meeting:

> *This meeting is assembled to bring home, if it is necessary to do so, the gravity of the crisis and the need for an effort*

unparalleled in our past history, because the circumstances calling for it are unparalleled. The claim upon the nation is one of honour, of interest, and national security. The final cause of our going to war is to vindicate the neutrality of Belgium ... In fighting this battle for Belgium we are also fighting against the new German theory that Germans are so much superior to the rest of the world that they may properly force upon them German ideas and the German standard of thought and cultivation in all relations of life, and that in the process of forcing that German standard of civilisation they may ignore the ordinary obligations that bind one man to another.

The badge of the Northamptonshire Regiment.

A variety of army men followed Lord Hugh onto the platform, each in his own way reminding the audience that they had an obligation to support the war effort. The Northamptonshire Regiment, of course, was well-represented and used the platform to reprise the regiment's past and the battle honours it had won. Applause from the audience was enthusiastic as they were reminded of Wellington's Peninsular campaigns, Talavera, Badajoz, Salamanca, the Crimea, the South African War and more recently, Aisne and Ypres:

No regiment has added more gloriously to its record in the war than the Northamptonshire Regiment. No better thing has been done in the war than the charge made by the 48th on the Aisne, when the regiment lost two of the best men who ever followed the Pytchley (hunt), Captains Parker and Russell.

At that the audience stood and cheered and clapped loudly. Support for the war, despite the constantly growing list of casualties published every week, was still as strong as ever. This was borne out by the rousing reception Edgar Mobbs received when he stood to bring the meeting to a close. Erudite, relaxed and at times humorous, he regaled everyone with amusing stories of his early life as a volunteer, how he had no understanding then of army systems or protocols, and how, to much laughter, that had brought him into conflict with those around him. But now he strongly supported the war and its aims, and crucially the reasons given as to why men should join. The whole event was a rousing success. Of course, how many were recruited as a result is unknown. But the meeting, like the recruitment march, was widely reported and many of those who wavered or had second thoughts probably reconsidered and formed an orderly queue outside the recruitment office over the coming weeks.

With men enlisting in huge numbers, not just in Northampton but across the country, the logistics of transport and housing for unprecedented numbers of soldiers was initially problematic, particularly when it came to billeting. But for Northampton, being a

The racecourse, which was used to train infantry, and later in the war to grow crops.

barracks town, and having housed the Welsh Division throughout the autumn and early winter of 1914 so successfully, continued billeting was never questioned. So, at the start of May, as news was released that a similar number of soldiers would be arriving before summer to take up the billets recently vacated, households around town began to prepare for another influx of strangers, though it's fair to say that having done it once, and having found the Welsh to be such excellent guests, any unwillingness to receive them was tempered by the positive experiences of the previous year.

The army too had learned from the experience. This time around, careful planning ensured the town was essentially split into a number of diverse areas, each area designated to a specific arm of the service. The Royal Army Medical Corps were quartered in houses around Kettering Road and East Park Parade. The Army Service Corps were at Kingsley. The Royal Field Artillery occupied homes nearest the racecourse. The Royal Engineers made use of homes nearest Market Square and the Corn Exchange. The main body of infantry were to move into houses around Kingsthorpe, the Wellingborough road area, the upper mounts, Cloutsham Street and numerous other terraced streets within reasonable proximity to the town. Far Cotton and St James were really the only exceptions because these areas were to be reserved for the new drafts that were posted from Cambridge every few weeks for short stays to take advantage of the nearby firing range. By early June, the first 5,000 men had already started arriving at Northampton railway station and been allocated to their appropriate area. It was a process that would continue throughout the war years.

As people digested the changes and began to accept the new routines foisted upon them by the military, there was little resentment. For most, the reshaping of their daily lives was readily embraced. Mindful of the army's need, and believing in the justness of the war they were now involved in, they simply carried on as normal. Daily routines, by and large, remained as they had always been. Across town, despite the uniforms and marching bands, work continued, as did the odd industrial dispute. Builders went on strike. Some 1,000 men downed tools after their demands for an extra penny an hour increase in wages was turned down. Something that had been bubbling up for weeks, it was short lived but effective. For a brief period, chaos reigned as all work associated with the building trade ground to a halt. Plumbers, carpenters, painters and decorators, roofers, bricklayers and numerous other trades walked off site. All domestic work was stopped, which meant that households were left without water in some cases, others with half-finished work on their homes. Anger mounted as the knock-on effect hit other industries. Then, as quickly as it had started, it ended and normality returned once more.

Not that it had had any real effect in the town's key industry. In the boot and shoe industries manufacturers were less concerned about wages and more concerned about retaining and protecting the staff they already had. Recruitment into the volunteer army had begun to affect the numbers employed, and was removing some skilled labour from various sectors. Those still working were under obvious pressure to join the fight and enlist in one of the services. Criticism of men who at this stage of the war had chosen to stay in employment rather than take up a uniform, had grown in intensity. Many were accosted in the street by people disapproving of their decision, regardless of age or perhaps infirmity. So, in order to assuage this censure, they created the War Badge. About the size of an old penny, generally worn on the sleeve, this was issued to workers bearing the name of the business that had issued it, and the words, 'On war service 1915'. The idea was to validate the work the wearer was involved in by identifying it as essential to the war effort. It was an idea that, as time passed, other industries also looked at using.

Equally essential to the war effort was, of course, the ability to treat the wounded. At the start of spring, Northampton's mayor appealed to both public and business institutions for more money for the hospital fund, capital so crucial if the town was to maintain the level of service it had striven to achieve throughout the first full year of war. Casualties were higher and more complex to deal with than had been imagined back in August 1914. They had also been more numerous than the hospital management committee had initially believed possible. The mayor told an audience of invited guests that they were already in a deficit position and would need fund-raisers working at a variety of events throughout the summer to help replenish the coffers. These events began on 9 May, a day chosen as Northampton's Hospital Sunday. This was a long-established event that had been ongoing for many years, but in 1915 there was an obvious need to exceed all previous targets. As he had told his audience people needed to contribute at levels they had never done before, and they did. The response by Northampton's residents was huge. Churches of all denominations held collections, businesses readily agreed to subscriptions and local people gave freely in the various street collections. Marching parades, brass bands and fancy dress competitions created a fun day and, for once, the weather worked in their favour. Elsewhere, similar events took place with many celebrating an annual hospital week in June, all following a similar format and all equally successful. The mayor's call for funds had been answered, and throughout it all the wounded continued to arrive in ever-increasing numbers.

This in turn meant that more hospital space was needed. Cottesbrooke Hall's original purpose had already been changed and

The entrance into the grounds of Cottesbrooke Hall.

further adapted and now had a capacity for 100 patients, to be cared for by four full-time nurses and four volunteer nurses, under the control of one sister and a full-time doctor. At the start of 1915, the hall was caring mainly for frostbite victims that had been brought in from Ypres. Of course, that changed as the year went on. Like Northampton Hospital, Cottesbrooke too suffered from lack of funding. The War Office paid the equivalent of 2 shillings a man per week to the hospital management, which was not enough. As casualties mounted, so donations were in constant demand throughout the war. To better cope with these wounded soldiers, Northampton continued to divide and allocate them as they arrived on the station platform depending upon their physical state and the nature of their wounds, as they had done in 1914. But by early summer all available beds were taken. An appeal from Southampton, which was where most of the wounded from France initially arrived, for Northampton to take more casualties was reluctantly refused. This decision caused argument and fierce debate amongst the town's medical teams, most of whom had been strongly opposed to the ruling made by the managing committee, believing that no casualty should be turned away. But it's hard to see how they could have made any other decision. At this point in the war, it would appear that casualties far outstripped the numbers originally thought would be arriving. What it did do was force a rethink. More buildings were eventually requisitioned under the powers granted to the government under the war act (DORA). This led to Kettering converting its sanatorium into a hospital along with Northampton's Berrywood Asylum, and as the years went by, various other places across the county were brought into use for the same purpose.

If, by this stage of the war, people had any doubts that the death toll was rising, then the *Northampton Mercury* dispelled them when it published Prime Minister Asquith's speech to the Commons from earlier in the year. According to the numbers he read out to the House of Commons, 104,000 British soldiers had become casualties before the start of spring, a number that everyone quickly realised was going to continue to rise, particularly as the wounded arriving in the town during May had arrived from battlegrounds at Ypres, Neuve Chapelle and Aubers Ridge. Places the newspapers had been reporting about since March and, on a more local level, regions where the Northamptonshire Regiment had been fighting. What was not known at the time, but is known today, is that at Neuve Chapelle the Northamptonshires suffered 432 casualties out of 616 men and at Aubers Ridge a further 426. Little wonder, then, that the weekly casualty lists throughout the first half of 1915 were constantly lengthening, with 170 losses in one week alone. Yet the newspapers continued to report 'glorious deeds from the front', as indeed they were expected to do. With no real representation on the front line to report first-hand experience throughout the whole war, it would have been difficult for them to have reported the army's actions in any other way. Unfortunately, realism and truth had been lost as a consequence of the government's refusal to allow factual reports to reach the public at home, unlike today. So, an acceptance by most that ever-lengthening casualty lists were a necessary by-product of modern warfare is perhaps

Northampton's Machine Gun Corps. (Northampton Central Library)

understandable. Even letters from the Front, which in many ways were extremely explicit, were published to reinforce the notion of a glorious war, often despite their content. But what they did do, as in the case of the one below from a private in the Northamptonshire Regiment, was to tell the truth behind the headlines:

> *Shells were falling like hailstones all the time. I had been hit very badly, a bullet going right through my jaw, shattering the bone and taking away all my teeth. The Germans had got within a few yards of our trenches. I was firing as quickly as ever I could and my mates were falling like ninepins from the enemy's fire. A party of Germans got round a slight hillock on our right and commanded a view of our trench from the end ... I dare not turn my attention on those as the Germans on the front were getting nearer and nearer every moment. Then I got it. I saw the chap who shot me ... I was unconscious for about five hours. Just a bandage round my wound was all the attention that could be given me for four days. And even when the RAMC tried to move us in motor vans the Germans attempted to blow us to pieces with shells. By good luck the Germans missed their target.*

Harrowing and honest. But back in May 1915, the biggest headlines of the day were for the sinking of the RMS *Lusitania*, a British ocean liner on route from New York to Liverpool that had been torpedoed and sunk by a German U-Boat 11 miles off the Irish coast. An act of infamy, at least that's how it was reported, and with some justification. A total of 1,198 passengers and crew died, including 128 Americans. The German submarine that sank the ship had absolutely no right to carry out the attack. It was against international laws and broke what was known as the cruiser rules that passenger ships were not to be sunk under any circumstances. There was a small number of Northampton families on board, whose photographs eventually appeared in the local newspapers. But perhaps more importantly, the attack itself reinforced the view that the war against Germany had to be fought to its conclusion.

In June, a second recruitment march was organised by the Northamptonshire Regiment. This time, after parading in the town's market square, and being inspected by Earl Spencer KC, Honorary Colonel, the regiment marched off along the Wellingborough Road, cheered on by huge crowds to the stirring tune of *Til the boys come home again*, played by the regimental band, their destination another week-long trek around the county then off to the barracks in St Albans. As before, they were met at every stopover by bands, flag-waving, cheering and patriotic songs. Local dignitaries gave rousing speeches and men flocked to the recruitment centres. It was another unqualified success.

Away from the war things were also changing. On 25 June, representatives of the Manufacturers Federation and National Union of Boot and Shoe Operatives signed what was known as a War

Emergency Agreement. In many ways this was a pivotal moment because, under its terms, women were allowed to perform certain operations within a factory that had previously been restricted to men. Furthermore, they were to be paid the same rate of pay as their male counterparts. Of course, it had come about because of the large numbers of men that were leaving the shoe industry to fight in France. But other industries too were beginning to change. In some cases, it was just allowing women more scope in the job market. In others, it was to change the very nature of the business itself.

Lloyd George made an appeal to the engineering industry in particular, to turn themselves into munitions factories. He wanted to create a scheme of what he termed, local national arsenals. The army needed an ever-increasing number of high-explosive shells, and the only way that was going to happen was if more premises were converted to munitions production:

David Lloyd George.

Plant a flag on your workshop. Every lathe you have got recruit it, enlist it.

This he told an audience in Cardiff, which was widely reported across the country, as he intended it to be. There was a growing need for such measures brought on by the manner in which the war was being fought and the length of time it seemed it was going to take to win it. For women in the town it meant another door would be opened into another industry that would pay well, so those working in the big houses around the town began to look elsewhere to earn. Shift-work in munitions factories paid far more than domestic work in town houses and the hours were more regular. The type of role played by women in the workplace was beginning to change and, as war progressed, these changes would manifest themselves across virtually every industry sector.

They would be needed, not just to keep the wheels of industry turning but also because women were set to become the chief, if not the only, wage-earner in the household. Generally, on the Home Front during 1915 food prices held. The price of wheat, in fact, fell dramatically at the start of the summer and, in turn, that brought down the price of bread. There had been no marked increase in the cost of clothing. Retail was operating pretty much along the same lines as pre-war, something that was not expected at the start of the year, and something unlikely to last as the war impacted more and more on imports as German submarines had an increasing impact on merchant shipping. August had been a very warm month, which proved fortuitous for the farmers. After a long spell of poor, wet weather they expressed concerns about the state of the crops in the fields. Autumn prices could have risen as a result. As it was the harvest was gathered throughout the month, though only with the help of the army, as the authorities released men onto the farms to help farmers hindered by lack of labour.

It had also been a good summer for the Sandbag Committee. This was operated primarily by the women of the town who produced sandbags for the Front. In order to fund the work, they raised monies by selling patriotic bows, flags and suchlike. This was much needed because it cost sixpence to produce one sandbag and, according to the

Berrywood as it looks today.

Loos, after the battle.

army, who reported back on quality, Northampton's sandbags were amongst the best.

Throughout the summer and early autumn, to help ease the strain on Northampton's hospital network, more conversion work was carried out at the Berrywood Asylum, which had been released earlier in the year for use by the military. It had been quickly realised that in order to meet the demand for beds, its capacity for treating wounded soldiers needed to be significantly increased. A contentious decision was, therefore, made to remove all the children still housed by the asylum and send them off to the workhouse. This decision was not without its critics but it did increase bed capacity, which ensured that the wounded would never again be turned away.

As that work concluded, news from the Front began to filter through about a major battle raging at a place named Loos, and losses were heavy. Casualty lists throughout October began to reflect this account with lists of the dead, wounded and missing being much higher than had been the norm. In turn, that increased the numbers of wounded arriving throughout the autumn.

Lists published by the *Northampton Mercury* were beginning to almost fill a complete page on a weekly basis, with losses for the Northamptonshire Regiment constantly seeming to increase, though it appears enthusiasm for the war was not tempered or in any way diminished. This was borne out by the fact that enlistment was still holding up despite these losses, and the disturbing war news coming out of Gallipoli where Turkey was fighting in support of Germany. For many, the war had settled perhaps into a sort of routine. News from the Front, a little detail about the fighting, lists of casualties and snippets of what was happening in town were the norm. Life generally appears to have carried on with a degree of regularity. What was clearly important was what happened to the wounded once they had arrived in Northampton.

Frequent reports came out from the hospitals concerning treatment and convalescence of the soldiers. Funding raised by locals bought comforts such as cigarettes, bed socks, dressing gowns, shirts and anything else deemed useful. During the warmer months, when they could sit out in the green areas, people, strangers, would visit, bring gifts and pass them cigarettes. When the darker nights came, concert

Wounded outside Northampton General Hospital. (Northampton Central Library)

parties were organised. In Northampton a group calling itself the Magnet Concert Party toured the shire. At each hospital they would sing the classics of the day, sometimes as soloists, or trios, and then get everyone singing along with the music hall hits that were in common parlance.

Anyone with a voice – nurse, doctor, soldier – was encouraged to use it, and they joined in readily. There's no doubt survival rates were good. Medical expertise over the space of a year or so had tremendously improved recovery rates, which continued to rise, as had the number of hospital beds available, particularly since the situation back in May when casualties were, in effect, being turned away. The complete re-appraisal of the town and county's ability to handle the numbers of wounded, that had in effect been ongoing throughout much of the year, had now come to an end. Overall, the changes were remarkable.

At the start of the war there were only 192 beds for the wounded in five key locations – Northampton General, Weston Favell hospital, Cottesbrooke Hall, Milton and Blakesley. Little change had been effected by the start of 1915. But by autumn of that year, there were 800 beds spread across seventeen locations, including Rushton Hall and Burghley House (in 1914 part of Northamptonshire), and that would reach 1,000 by year-end. The town could also call on five ambulances, which meant that through the year it had taken in a total of 2,117 wounded cases from Dover and Southampton, the main receiving ports for those wounded at the Front, along with 500 patients transferred in from Cambridge. A considerable success from how the year had begun.

But it was not just soldiers that needed help. The annual meeting of Northampton's branch of the Royal Society for the Prevention of Cruelty to Animals was held at the Town Hall, principally to discuss the situation of horses being drawn into the army for service abroad. They also wanted to organise a flag day to collect funds in aid of horses that had been injured or wounded at the Front. Having run an event in Bedford, where they raised £400, it seemed an obvious mechanism for funding their work on the continent. Impressing horses into the army had been ongoing since the start of the war. Across Northampton,

Rushton Hall used for wounded soldiers throughout the war.

farmers, local businesses, stables and private owners had given up their animals under the terms of the Army Act, mainly due to the fact that horses were the only means of transport for a variety of branches of the services. They pulled the gun carriages, the ambulances, carried ammunition, and were, of course, used by the cavalry. Mechanised transport had limited use around the front line, ground conditions were pretty atrocious for much of the time due to the lack of drainage. Land around the front lines was sodden for much of the year, making movement extremely difficult. So the army made it a rule that anything going towards the firing line had to be carried by horses for the last 5 miles, resulting in an incredible loss of life.

This in turn meant more and more horses being sourced from the mainland, and eventually America and Canada. Horses from across the whole county had been, and were, constantly being recruited for service in the army, although the rule was that every animal impressed into

Veterinary hospital in France.

service had to be bought at the prevalent market price. It was little compensation for those who had to give them up. What the society wanted to do was try and ensure that those horses collected at the cattle market had access to proper veterinary services. They also wanted to carry this caring policy to the front line, where they had begun to have some success. In the previous year they had published and distributed amongst those in the army's equine service over 55,000 booklets on how to care for horses, and sent volunteers into front line areas to set up temporary horse shelters. They also built a horse hospital in Northern France to accommodate 1,000 horses, all of which needed funding. So, the idea of a flag day was agreed for the following year, as was trying to raise funds through Northampton churches and possibly some street collections, not easy at this stage of the war when many were contributing to the war effort through a variety of other funds and collections. Nevertheless, they were intent on trying. They knew at this stage something the town did not, just how difficult life on the Front was for horses, most of whom had obviously never seen action, heard a gun fired or been forced to work in such terrible conditions as were prevalent all along the front line. The RSPCA had also been working with local farmers to buy sheepskins, which were used to bind around parts of the harness to prevent rubbing sores.

Lobbying at government levels also forced the authorities to recognise the society and the work it was engaged in. In turn, this meant they were able to link up with the Army Veterinary Department and create eighty horse ambulances to carry wounded animals away from the front line. An organisation much needed and much underrated.

By the end of October, the *Northampton Mercury* reported the introduction of the Derby Scheme. Instigated by Lord Derby (Edward Stanley), director general of recruiting, its supposed intent was to prevent forcible conscription. After the implementation of the National Registration Act back in May, which forced every man to register his employment, the government had an overview by the end of 1915 of just how many men were working in industries that would require their skill-base throughout the war. Those men would eventually become exempt, in other words not eligible for enlistment. Keeping key industries at full capacity was obviously as essential as keeping the armed forces at full strength. By autumn, having gathered this information, government policy toward volunteering was then directed at all those not in essential war work. This was the intention of Derby's scheme.

Under its provisions, all men between the ages of 18 and 40 were told they could either enlist voluntarily and go off to war with immediate effect, or attest (commit to join at a later date), with an obligation to become a part of the fighting army at a date set in the future. Those who attested and were accepted medically but chose to defer their join up were categorised as being Class A. They were paid a day's army pay on the day they attested, given a grey armband to wear as a sign that they had volunteered, and were transferred administratively into Section B of the army reserve then sent home. Those who did enlist straight away were in Class B. Those who attested were then broken down into married or single status. There were twenty-three groups for the single men and twenty-three groups for the married men. These were all based on age. For example, a single man aged 18 was in Group 1; a single man aged 40 was in Group 23. It worked in exactly the same way for married men but, because it was intended that all single men would be called on first, 18-year-old married men were in Group 24, while 40-year-old married men were in Group 46. Under the scheme, these groups were then called to enlist throughout 1916. Groups 1 to 5, for example, had to report to the recruitment office at the end of January, groups 6 to 13 in February, and so on. It meant that the army always knew how many men were set to join the ranks at any one time and could easily calculate the future strength of the fighting force it had access to.

A flurry of meetings took place in Northampton throughout November in an attempt to explain this rather complicated process to both workers and employers. Confusion reigned as everyone tried to get a grip on just exactly what was meant by the whole process and the effect it was likely to have on the town. To facilitate its implementation, Northampton employed a team of canvassers. Their role was to visit every man within the 18 to 40 age range and get them to enrol in the scheme, regardless of occupation. They then reported back to a number of recruitment committees that were set up to monitor and manage the process. But there were areas of real confusion. Employers employing men on government work, munitions, engineering, and so on, had by this time adopted and issued them with badges that they all wore to identify them as being involved in crucial work. These badges, it had been decided by the government, would exempt them from military service. The job would be starred (exempted). But under the scheme these men still had to enrol. The argument put forward by Lord Derby was that despite the badge they could still resign their post and take up a gun:

> *It does not follow, however that they are exempt from enrolment. The man who has the badge may leave his present employment a month hence and lose his qualification for the badge.*

At a meeting of manufacturers and tradesmen held at the Town Hall to discuss this point and others, it was pointed out by many that a number of employers had given a patriotic pledge to keep positions open for men who had enlisted, and also to pay families part-wages while these men were on active service. But if more employees were to be forced to enlist, these companies would find it difficult to carry out these obligations. Trade would be affected adversely, profits would fall and

Soldiers of the Northamptonshire Regiment helping out at harvest time. (Northampton Central Library)

there would be less capital available to continue an agreement so honestly made. Also, it appeared railwaymen, who by the nature of their work were all working for the government, had been offered no protection at all. Clearly there were anomalies, not that it changed anything. The scheme was rolled out across town and county throughout November, with a final push to increase the numbers during the first half of December. But overall it was a failure. Despite the numbers who did enrol many did not. The days of being able to create an army purely on a voluntary basis were numbered, and as losses continued to mount, it would finally come to an end early in 1916.

While this debate was raging, what was known as the County War Agricultural Committee was meeting at Northampton's cattle market. Farmers, as we already know, had had a tough year. Not through crop failure or a decline in profits, but through a lack of manpower, which in essence meant that those working on the land had seen an increase in their workload just to maintain the status quo.

The knock-on effect was that farmers, who had predicted all this back in the spring when they had made the request to recruit 12-year-olds, had not been able to increase yields at a time when demands on the food supply chain were at their highest, and now found themselves under increasing government pressure, with much of their skilled labour, as discussed at that spring meeting, having been absorbed into the army. The committee had come together because harvesting in 1915 had been extremely problematic. Farms had to call on Northampton's army barracks to provide labour in order to ensure the summer crop was gathered before the weather turned. The situation, they warned, would worsen if this labour shortage could not be rectified. In a full and frank exchange of views, the key point was not a concern about the impact of Lord Derby's scheme on agriculture, as most eligible men had already left the industry. It was how the town expected them to move forward into 1916 increasing productivity, which they readily accepted was necessary, without the manpower to facilitate such an increase. To continue growing food and producing meat for the table they needed access to labour, even if only temporary, on a more continuous basis.

According to the *Northampton Mercury*, who reported the meeting, the discussions once again centred around employing women, and boys of 12. In Parliament, Lord Selbourne, president of the Board of Agriculture, had already been widely reported as being strongly in favour of more women being brought into farming if the industry was to meet the future demands that would inevitably be made upon it. They were already working in farms all across Scotland. But this was not a policy Northampton's farmers agreed. When raised during the discussions it met with outright refusal yet again, though not necessarily on the grounds of sexism. Most felt that the women of Northampton, both town and shire, would not welcome farm-work. Pay, they pointed out, was generally poor and most farmers subscribed to the opinion that most women viewed farm-work as a step too far. It was felt strongly that even if the farmers would accept women labouring on the land, it was doubtful they would join the agricultural ranks in sufficient numbers to make any serious impact. Of course it was total nonsense, as the later war years were to prove. But this was a physical, arduous, male-dominated industry that had never numbered many women amongst its labour force. To contemplate such a radical change to the farming operation was no doubt extremely difficult for many to even consider. Nevertheless, they were all realists and recognised that unless the war suddenly ended, they would be forced to change their views. To that end, it was agreed to begin canvasing the views of women. In the meantime, to solve the immediate problem of farm labour shortage, men of the Northamptonshire Regiment, not just boys of school age, would be released to work on the land for the four weeks of December. The army also agreed that while a better solution was being sought they would provide limited labour throughout the following year. All that was required of the farmer was that he give at least twenty-four hours' notice. This resolution at least satisfied the meeting, although, as the local paper reported, it still did nothing to facilitate farms releasing more land to grow cereal crops. Without a guaranteed workforce in place an increase in productivity would be meaningless if it could not be properly harvested.

In fact, adequate food production was beginning to cause some real concern in the town as the year drew to a close. The national press had raised it as an issue at the end of the summer and, as the local newspapers began to discuss the issues, there was real concern that prices would climb in 1916. There was also concern in the town about education. Teachers were in short supply. Many had already enlisted and there was now insufficient teaching staff in many places. Throughout the year the council had already been grouping schools together, which essentially meant sharing staff. But even that was becoming difficult, and moves were afoot to begin a programme of school closures. Most small schools were at risk and, in light of the farmers' labour problems, the education committee, despite earlier reservations, was beginning to form the view that perhaps releasing these boys at 12, allowing them to go and work on the land, would also help cut the student population. Perhaps, they argued, it really was no bad thing if schools were going to be either cut in size or closed permanently.

Lots of issues, lots of concerns. Christmas in Northampton in 1915 was, perhaps understandably, a subdued affair. The streets were quiet, celebrations low key. Families were coping with more and more as the year had progressed. Publicity surrounding the Lord Derby scheme and all its implications, casualty lists growing ever longer, lower food production, worries over prices and growing concerns over Zeppelin raids, these things obviously had an effect. But if the town struggled with Christmas, the hospitals did not. All the wounded were given a gift of a leather wallet, containing a notebook, a Christmas card signed by the mayor, and a pack of cigarettes. In Northampton General the nurses donned their capes, carried lanterns around the wards and sang carols. For those worried about life at the Front there was also a little reassurance. It came in the form of a letter published by the *Northampton Mercury* from Northampton soldier, Sergeant Pettit:

> *I find that people at home have somehow a wrong idea of the life of the men out at the front. They think it is all muddy trenches and sudden death, and that sort of thing. There is enough, and more than enough, of that, of course, but there is a good deal of fun and merriment. Indeed I think I can honestly say that during the last five months I have spent some of the jolliest times of my life. The original D Company were like a lot of schoolboys together. A good number of them like myself ... There was that spirit about all our training and we carried it over to France. The Company has changed a lot of course lately, but the drafts have all been jolly good chaps and I should say, certainly with regard to the thirty per cent or thereabouts of the originals who are left, no body of men could have better times together.*

CHAPTER 3

1916
The Realities of War

The new year dawned with news that courses in economical cooking were to be launched in Northampton. It had been decided that as a result of the impeding food shortages and increases in cost, families would have to learn how to eat a different diet. It's fair to say that, unlike today, not a lot was known about food at this time. For many, up until this point in the war, diet had been reasonably good, maybe not varied but with food quality generally of a high standard that mattered little. What was proposed in January 1916 was that habits may be forced to change. It was argued that there now needed to be a level of economy in the selection and preparation of food. Cheaper foodstuffs, which had become the staple diet of most households, were at risk. Housewives, it was felt, had to learn how to get more benefit from the food they bought at less cost.

Northampton's education committee had been looking at ways of re-educating women in how to make their money go further, and how to cook in a different way. Cookery classes were considered to be the best way of doing that. With the war now unlikely to end in the near future, the Royal Navy's capacity to maintain open shipping channels for imports stretched to the limit, and farmers currently unable to increase their crop yields, families would be forced to change long-held traditions and habits. Women, particularly those with children,

Woman learning new cooking methods.

had become pillars of family life. They were under pressure from all quarters. In many households there was no longer any shared responsibility, it was all theirs. Husbands and sons at the Front meant not only was there the worry about loved ones never returning, but there was also the huge responsibility of running the house and managing its running costs. That included not only the cooking, cleaning, shopping and schooling, but also paying the bills and, in some cases, holding down a job. So it was vital that they understood they could provide for their families on lower incomes by shopping wisely, buying lower grade food and cooking it attractively and nutritiously.

Meanwhile, the fundraising that had been in operation in the run-up to Christmas bought significant goods for the troops. The boot manufacturers and local shopkeepers managed to raise £24 that had been turned into an impressive list of goods (shown below), all of which had arrived on the front line in time for Christmas day:

8,000 cigarettes
112 one ounce packets of Glasgow smoking mixture and some
   clay pipes
24 doz packets of safety matches
24 doz Oxo cubes
24 mouth organs
15 doz pairs of leather laces
24 doz boxes of Dubbin
6 doz packets of soap
18lb Brazil nuts
8lb chocolate
6 doz song sheets
6 doz boxes of Vaseline
2 doz tins of Keatings (powder to kill fleas)
48 doz candles

Clearly, £24 bought a lot, all of it useful. Other organisations raised similar amounts and probably provided a similar list of goods. People quickly realised more would be needed as the year progressed. On 4 January 1916, Prime Minister Asquith introduced the Military Service Bill. Essentially conscription for all men between the ages of 18 to 40, the only exemptions were for those in holy orders and those who had already been rejected on medical grounds. Kitchener came out in support:

> *It only affected one class of men, amongst whom there were undoubtedly a certain number who had but a poor idea of their duties as citizens and required some persuasion greater than appeal to bring them to the colours.*

Soldiers after arriving in France.

What he meant here was that, to date, it had been either patriotism or the scheme set up by Lord Derby that had prevailed. Namely that the army was a voluntary service and could no longer be sustained on that basis. Obviously, the loss of life meant the front line had to be continually replenished with new troops. When the *Northampton Mercury* published yet another list of casualties, this time from the Battle at Loos the previous September, it was pretty obvious for any doubters to understand the tenure of his argument:

Officers killed	773
Officers wounded	1,288
Officers missing	317
Other ranks killed	10,345
Other ranks wounded	38,095
Other ranks missing	8,848
Total casualties	59 666

Sobering news from the front line. Any lingering doubts that this was a war with no end in sight were probably dispelled by the combination of these numbers and the imposition of conscription.

On a more positive note, Northampton's shoe trade was very much on the up along with wages. Already supplying Britain and much of the French Army's footwear, it received a request from the Italian government to supply them also with between 150,000 and 200,000 pairs of boots. Their own supplies had failed because they had found it difficult to source the heavy nails needed to produce a robust boot that would withstand the rigours of an army at war. Italy was not at war with Germany at this stage. She had intended to remain neutral and had succeeded in this until May 1915, when the lure of territorial gains and money plus equipment from the Allies had caused a rethink, and she had declared war upon Austria in order to gain Trieste. This meant that the decision for the shoe manufacturers to supply the boots was not automatic. But after a meeting of Northampton manufacturers, it was decided that provided supplying the Italians did not adversely affect supplies to the Western Front, they would agree to the request. No doubt there had also been a degree of pressure from elsewhere to comply, mainly because the Allies wanted Italy in the war, although they had to wait until August before the Italians finally declared war against Germany. Nevertheless, for the industry in Northampton, it was a major boost to an already booming business.

This was obviously good news for the town and all those employed in the industry, but what most families were after was more news from the Front. It had been a quiet period with seemingly little activity and even less information filtering out to folk at home. So, when Edgar Mobbs, now a captain, slipped back into Northampton in the early hours of 6 January, it quickly became headline news. Locals and press alike sought him out. Back for a week on home leave and well aware that people would want to talk with him, he agreed to meet reporters between visits to the homes of those in the regiment that had served with him and been killed. Time to talk was somewhat limited. Nevertheless, he was willing to make himself available and met with the *Mercury*'s reporter a couple of days after his arrival. Upbeat and obviously glad to be back home, he told the newspaper that all was well in France, and that the men from the town were all doing well after having a reasonably good Christmas:

We had an excellent Christmas in billets – barns and places of that character. There was extra fare for the men – plum puddings ... and many other gifts from Northampton, and in the afternoon there was an association football match in which the men beat the offices by four goals to one.

He went on to explain that the reason for visiting soldiers' families while he was home was not just to explain the circumstances around their loved ones' deaths. It was also to let the families know that after the Battle of Loos, which is where most of the losses occurred, he and others from the regiment had found a damaged church. Outside that church they had created a graveyard for the Northamptonshires and buried as many of the dead as they were able. Each grave had its own cross and on every grave an empty Perrier bottle, inside which was placed the man's name, regimental number, date killed and manner in which he met his death:

We wired the ground off and put up a notice board showing that the space is the burial ground of men of the Northamptonshire Regiment, and in years to come the friends of some of the men who lay there will be able to identify the spot where one they loved and whose memory they cherish is resting.

Before he left to return to France, Edgar Mobbs was promoted to temporary major.

On his return to the Front he probably found little had changed. The armies were in stalemate and waiting for spring. Back in Northampton, with the onset of winter and the escalating fear about air-raids, things were changing. Mid-January saw the introduction of what was known as the New Lighting Order. In an attempt to minimise the opportunities for Zeppelin attacks it had been decided that, in addition to the dimming of street lights, which had been the practice since the previous year, all other lighting was to be severely restricted. This meant, as part of those restrictions, all vehicles on the road had to cut down the

Zeppelin caught in the searchlights.

amount of light emitted from headlights. In essence that meant cars were driven by the light of small lamps, which in turn restricted their speed and rendered them almost useless for travel at night. Shops, factories and public buildings had to shade their windows, and all homes had to hang dark curtains or blinds to block out all light. No exceptions were allowed. Furthermore, police were instructed to rigorously enforce the new regulations and prosecute any that ignored the dictate. Judging by the court cases reported, a fair number initially failed to react fast enough. By the end of the month, fifty-eight had been summoned and a further 100 prosecutions were in the pipeline and, according to police, more were likely to follow.

With fines ranging from around 10 shillings (50p) to one pound and the courts having the latitude to increase the level, it was to prove costly for some. But when the air-raid sirens sounded at 9pm on 31 January, as the first major Zeppelin raid of the war began, many realised the merit of total darkness. Across Northampton every street light was extinguished. Gas pressures were lowered, all trains were stopped, traffic on all roads brought to a halt and cinemas and theatres quickly closed. Unfortunately, the sound of engines high above the town also brought people out onto the streets, curiosity being the main reason for coming out on a cold night. For the sake of safety, police reacted by sending out an additional fifty special constables. According to Bette Davis, writing many years after the event:

> There was nothing to be seen really. Just the noise and that was far off from where we were stood. But people were really excited. Course we had no idea about bombs and suchlike.

Twenty-four hours later they knew all too well. News reports circulated about the destruction that had caused the deaths of fifty-nine men, women and children across the east coast, Lincolnshire, Leicestershire, Derbyshire and Staffordshire, along with 101 wounded after 300 bombs were dropped. Dimming the lights after that probably seemed a small price to pay for safety.

Bombing, of course, would become more frequent in parts of the country as the war progressed, and like many other aspects of this war, people would grow more used to it. By March, fear of it had already begun to fade into the background. More newsworthy by far was the growing number of what were often termed 'conscientious objectors' appearing before the appeals tribunal held at Northampton's County Hall. At this stage of the war the term conscientious objector, widely used by the local press, did have a slightly different connotation than it would have later. In March 1916, the term tended to always be applied to a serving soldier who had enlisted then refused to take up arms. These men faced a court-martial, often held at the church institute in Kingsthorpe. Civilians, often classified under the same heading, were generally individuals who had joined the Derby Scheme at the end of 1915, but then wanted to opt out as the army called them into service. These men were brought before an appeals tribunal to argue their case against enlistment. Generally, this was on the grounds of performing work of national importance or, through family hardship. This began to change after the Conscription Act had become law in late March. The Act included a conscience clause whereby any man who had a conscientious objection to bearing arms could be freed from military service. So the panel that sat in judgement from that time onward had a different intent from its predecessor. These panels, made up largely of businessmen, retired military officers, civil servants and always one serving army officer, were hugely patriotic with, of course, one remit – fill the depleted ranks with more men. Those that came before them generally appealed against serving on medical grounds, religious grounds or war-work, farming and the like. The panel often viewed them as belonging to one of three groups: abolutionists, those opposed to war; alternativists, those prepared to do civilian work; and non-combatants, those prepared to enlist but not to fight. It's fair to say that most who appeared before the Northampton panels certainly got the opportunity of stating their case. What they probably did not get was a sympathetic ear.

As March drew to a close even the widely reported proceedings of this court were overtaken by nature. Reported as 'The Great Storm', it hit the town at the end of the month with devastating effect. Heavy snow fell for twenty-two hours. Blown in on gale-force winds from the east, it brought down chimneys, telephone and telegraph wires, parts

Northamptonshire Women's Institute.

of the railway station, and hundreds of trees. Forty-eight hours after the storm, the town was essentially cut off. All trains were stopped, villages were inaccessible as all roads in and out were blocked, the roofs of shops, houses and businesses were weighed down by up to 2 feet of snow, and in places snowdrifts up to 10 feet deep. Essentially, all movement around town ground to a halt. According to the *Northampton Mercury*, industry was brought to a standstill, and across the county it was even worse. A warming sun caused a melt, which in turn caused widespread flooding. The River Nene burst its banks in places and, as travel became easier around town, it became impossible in other parts of the county.

The chaos, of course, was only temporary. But its impact, no matter how short-lived, did affect people's lives. Throughout this brief period food supplies dwindled. Afterwards they were slow to be replenished. Food prices were still rising and by spring there were signs that it would be a difficult summer. German submarines were having a greater impact on merchant shipping than had been thought possible at the start of the year. Supplies of imported foodstuffs were diminishing and stocks were becoming depleted. More land was needed, to turn over to food crop production. Despite a reasonable harvest in the autumn of 1915, wheat stocks in Britain by the end of April were down to six weeks' supply. Shortages meant people had to look at other ways of growing food. In Northampton, part of the racecourse was turned into allotments. Back gardens became vegetable patches and pressure was put onto the farming community to increase crop yields.

This in turn re-ignited the argument that had been raging since early in the war, that more women were needed in agriculture and more farmers had to accept them into their labour force, particularly after the results of the survey carried out by the Agricultural Committee at the end of the previous year had actually shown little resistance to the idea by women themselves. By this stage of the war they had already, despite fierce opposition at times, managed to move successfully into a cross-section of industries. The suffragette movement, if it had done nothing else, had propagated a belief amongst many women that their status in society was already changing. The Home Front would create ever-increasing opportunities to enhance it even further. What they now wanted was more freedom, more recognition of their worth, and less opposition from men as they sought a place in the country's workforce. They had done the knitting, organised the fundraising, done the good works and the voluntary roles. What they were beginning to demand at this stage of the war was public recognition for what they had done so far and what they could further achieve.

At a meeting held at the Town Hall, presided over by the lady mayoress, Mrs Pearse, and supported by the chairwoman of the County Women Workers Committee, Lady Knightley, an audience predominately made up of local women was told what the town had finally decided about agriculture. Essentially, the idea was that the county be divided into twelve distinct districts, each district to contain nineteen or twenty villages, each with an appointed representative of the union and a registrar. Their task was to identify the farms in need of labour, and draw up a list of the women within the district prepared to work on the land.

To facilitate an easier transition from factory or office-based occupations to agricultural work, a training course was set-up at what was called the County Experimental Farm at Moulton. The course would run for a period of four weeks. Accommodation would be provided for six women each month, and all would be taught the rudiments of farming. The down-side was that the course cost £3, but

Women at work.

this money would be eventually returned in the form of a 15-shilling allowance (75p) for food. Once they had passed the course they would be employed by farmers on wages of between 18 shillings (90p) and one pound per week for an average eight-hour day, usually provided with lodgings on site and, in some cases, including meals. Clothing in

Women by this time were involved in most aspects of work once the domain of men.

the form of breeches and leggings, a loose coat or smock, and either a felt hat or woollen cap were also provided. The idea had already gone down well with most farmers because it removed the worries attached to employing unskilled labour along with the cost of having to train women on site. It was a positive step forward and warmly received by the attentive audience in Northampton.

It was a plan that worked to varying degrees and, over the coming months, more and more women did take up roles working on farms. In turn this allowed farmers who had been resistant since the outset of war to employ these women in various roles, to better manage the land, though it did not remove the problem of replacing the skills that had been lost in areas of stock management, breeding, handling key pieces of farming machinery and the like: that would take longer to achieve. In fact, for many, those kinds of issues were not really resolved until the formation of the Women's Land Army in 1917.

But as one problem seemed to be solved, another began to rear its head. In May 1916, 1,000 boys and 500 girls employed in the boot and shoe industry downed tools and went on strike. Almost every factory across town was brought to a halt, mainly due to the fact that their refusal to work meant that those in the lasting and finishing

Moulton Agricultural College, which played a key role in training women to work on the land.

departments of these factories could not complete their assigned tasks and so the whole factory was brought to a standstill. As non-members of the union, because of their age but no doubt with union support, they were seeking parity with the general workforce, namely the receipt of a war bonus. This bonus was already in existence and paid to all employees over the age of 18, and they felt it ought to be paid to them also. The average wage for boys under 18 was between 22 shillings (£1.10p) and 28 shillings (£1.40p) per week. Adding a bonus, which certainly would not have amounted to much extra, was a contentious issue. It caused widespread anger amongst those whose jobs had been brought to a halt, and as a consequence caused a cut in their pay. For others it became a point of principle. The president of the Manufacturers' Association, Mr Marlow, travelled from Northampton to London to meet War Office officials and apprise them of the situation. Strikes in the industry were not well-received at government level. They wanted a resolution and they wanted it fast. Meanwhile, at the Trade Hall in Northampton, the men who had been thrown out of work as a consequence of what they saw as an unnecessary strike demanded the union pay them what was known as 'lock out pay'. The union in turn asked for their support in backing the action, something they were not willing to do. Angry scenes followed. Union officials who tried to calm the situation were shouted down and the meeting became extremely chaotic. Men, at risk of being impoverished by a strike they had never sought, demanded the youngsters return to work. It was put to the vote and they won the day. The strike was stopped and, by the end of a week of strife, normality returned to the shoe industry.

Elsewhere, the first half of 1916 passed relatively peacefully, with no other serious strikes. The introduction of the Daylight Saving Act, which caused the clocks to go forward an hour, had generated some consternation but was otherwise accepted. Supplies of coal became spasmodic and more expensive, though it was hoped that moving the clocks would help reduce coal usage, both in industry and the home. Military authorities, under the power granted to them through the Defence of the Realm Act, seized all the hay and straw brought to market in Northampton. Under the Act it could not be sold privately without the granting of a permit. In early spring farmers had been selling at over £8 a ton. The authorities wanted to bring the price down and control the markets, seizing these commodities and then releasing them back to market, through the Northamptonshire's Forage Committee, and had pulled those high prices back below the £6 a ton threshold, which was where they wanted them. Elsewhere, it was bread that steadily increased in price and became an issue for many households, with frequent queues forming outside bakeries. Sugar was also difficult to obtain, mainly due to a reduction in imports.

All the soldiers billeted across town had left. Marching to the railway station, behind their regimental band, they were put on a series of trains that ferried them south and eventually across the Channel. As summer dawned, the town fell quieter than it had been for months. But if people thought life was difficult at home, they only had to read Private George Wells' letter, published by the local press, to see how difficult life could become. George had been employed in the shoe factory at Kingsthorpe before the war and joined up at the outset, arriving in France in September 1914, but he'd been captured a month later. What happened to him after that made harrowing reading:

> *Hard work and scanty rations combined played havoc with us, and we suffered terribly from the intense cold, many dying. For over six months they never allowed me to write home or receive parcels. I never had a change of shirt for more than six months. The Germans took a delight in keeping us short of clothing as well as food, and they went so far as to take away our overcoats despite the severity of the winter.*

What they also never provided were boots and so, throughout the winter of his incarceration, he was barefoot. Only after the capture of some British doctors, who were brought to the camp, did he receive any medical attention, but the end result was gangrene and an operation to amputate much of both feet. His diet after surgery during the remainder of his stay in prison was extremely poor:

> *Bill-posters paste – bran, potatoes, maize gruel and black bread, which was not conducive to a speedy recovery.*

This, he believed, was disastrous for many of the soldiers captured and only changed toward the end of 1915:

> *The American Ambassador at Berlin (Mr Gerard) made a thorough personal inspection. After this more fire and food were allowed together with facilities for communicating with friends and receiving parcels, but throughout the whole of the time the German officials openly displayed their particular aversion for British prisoners and lost no time in treating them worse than the French and the Russian.*

These postcards were commonplace in commemoration of Lord Kitchener after his death at sea.

Eventually, George was invalided home and he went on to have artificial feet fitted at the military hospital in Roehampton. Clearly, things at home could have been much worse. Then came news of the death of Lord Kitchener.

Newspapers reported that he had been killed after the ship, HMS *Hampshire*, taking him to Russia and a planned meeting with the Czar, had struck a mine 1½ miles north-west of the Orkneys. He, his staff and most of the ship's crew, around 650 men, were drowned in rough sea. A cult figure, whose face adorned thousands of recruitment posters, Lord Kitchener was much revered by many as the hero of the empire. There was a sense of shock but no time to mourn. As news of his fate broke, so did the losses after the biggest naval battle of the war at Jutland. Newspapers were suddenly full of photographs of Northampton sailors killed in action on the high seas, men like 17-year-old telegraphist Able Seaman Smith serving on HMS *Invincible*, which sunk with the loss of over 1,000 men, Leading Stoker William Northcote, among the 1,200 men killed on HMS *Queen Mary*, and Lieutenant Frederick Cook, who died on HMS *Hampshire*, along with

Lord Kitchener. The list grew longer as the days passed. Because of the restrictions placed on press reporting at the time, it was impossible for people to know whether this was victory or defeat. The casualty list suggested the latter, but the presented facts pointed to a successful naval engagement. It was only after the war people realised that, in total, over 6,500 British sailors lost their lives. On the plus side, though again not realised at the time, the battle sent the German Navy back to port and there it stayed for the remainder of the war.

As the people were beginning to digest this information news broke of a major offensive by the British and French armies at the Somme. The French commander, Joffre, having seen the French and German armies fight themselves to a standstill at Verdun (a battle that had been raging for five months by July 1916), proposed a new offensive at the place where the British and French armies met on the River Somme. Douglas Haig, who had taken over command of the Allied army from Sir John French after the slaughter at Loos, agreed. The plan was to launch a massive assault against the Germans that would bring the war to an end. It was a disaster. History now records it as the bloodiest battle in the history of warfare.

On 1 July 1916, casualties totalled 60,000, and when the battle finally drew to a close at the end of November, 142 days later, the Allied casualties had grown to 420,000, for no real gain. The 1st Battalion Northamptonshire Regiment fought at Albert, Bazentin Ridge, Pozieres, Flers-Courcelette and Morval. The 2nd Battalion also at Albert and also Vimy Ridge. The lengthening casualty lists, in places accompanied by photographs of soldiers killed and poignant obituaries, filled the local newspapers, reflected the disaster. Not that it was reported in any way with a negative slant, but the evidence was there for all to see. Numerous Northampton families lost fathers, sons and husbands through the summer and early autumn of 1916.

On the plus side, the Somme was the first battle to use tanks, or land dreadnoughts as the press initially referred to them. These machines would eventually turn the tide of war. But in 1916 their real value was not recognised by all the generals and, to be fair, they were not hugely

HMS Hampshire, the ship carrying Lord Kitchener when it struck a mine.

successful. Of the thirty-two used at the Somme only nine managed to navigate their way across No-Man's-Land. Nevertheless, the potential was there and, to the army's credit, they did not abandon the idea that a mobile, mechanised weapon of this type could eventually prove extremely useful, as it did a year later.

In September 1916, the town turned out *en masse* to meet the Northamptonshire Regiment's Sergeant William Boulter, who had been awarded the Victoria Cross in July. He arrived by train with his mother and father and, after greeting the waiting crowds, they were all taken to the Abington Road branch of the Co-operative Society, where he was presented with a clock on behalf of all the employees. Then on to the Franklin's Hotel, on Guildhall Road for lunch, before being taken to the army barracks, where he and his family and friends joined a parade that marched them down to Abington Park. There, a platform had been erected where he was greeted by the mayor, deputy mayor, the mayor's chaplain, all the town council, the town's magistrates and numerous other dignitaries. Bands played, people cheered and the army turned out in force. Sergeant Boulter, for a day at least, was a celebrity, and Northampton was proud. Not that he was the town's first Victoria Cross winner. That honour had gone to Captain Anketell Read, a former heavyweight boxing champion, back in 1915, but unfortunately he had not survived his wounds. So the town wanted to take the opportunity, not often afforded those attaining the highest military award, of celebrating not only Sergeant Boulter's bravery but also his good fortune. It was a thank you on a huge scale. For William Boulter, it was all probably a little overwhelming but richly deserved. When he addressed the crowd of well-wishers that applauded him as he arrived, and cheered him as he spoke, his message was simple and no doubt heartfelt:

> *I hardly know how to thank you. . . for the warm reception you have given me. I shall always treasure it, and it will bring me pleasant memories. I only went out to do my bit the same as others, and I hope I have succeeded. I hope that co-operation will bring about a better feeling among the people and that in future there will be no more terrible wars brought about by one or two people.*

Thankfully, he did survive the war.

Cheering news reached Northampton at the start of winter, after reports reached the town of the destruction of a Zeppelin south of the county. A Northamptonshire soldier in the Royal Flying Corps, in a letter to his mother, Mrs Quincey, which was subsequently published, described how it had been attacked from the air:

> *When I looked out of the bedroom window there was a Zeppelin floating over the top of us. It went on, and then turned and came back in our direction. We could see the Zepp coming on and the shells bursting, and then I saw a small tongue of flame leap from the Zepp. Like someone striking a match, and that was the beginning of the end, for it suddenly burst into a big flame and began to fall. Then the blaze broke out and lit the place up by day. You could see to read a paper for about five minutes, until she finally hit the earth and then there was a terrific explosion. It was a sight never to be forgotten. When she caught properly afire the hand-clapping, shouting, cheering, and women crying was enough to deafen you.*

What he was describing was the air attack by RFC pilot, Lieutenant William Leefe Robinson, which completely destroyed the airship and

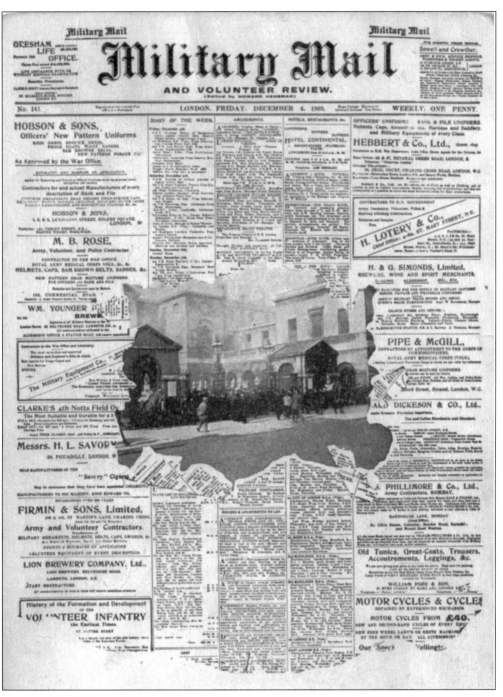

The Military Mail and Volunteer Review used by the services, this one is prior to the outbreak of war.

earned him a Victoria Cross. The Zeppelin's crew were all killed and later given a full military funeral, attended by a number of pilots from the Flying Corps. Parts of the Zeppelin were later collected and sold by the Red Cross to raise funds for wounded soldiers.

As big and clumsy-looking as Zeppelins were, they had proven extremely difficult to destroy and had wreaked havoc across the country. Bits of an airship, once thought invulnerable, were no doubt highly saleable. Certainly to those living with the blackouts in Northampton the destruction of one was extremely well-received.

But the Western Front and what was happening there was never far from the news. Throughout the summer, with casualty lists growing, there had been a concerted effort not just in Northampton but across the whole county to raise more and more funds, either for the soldiers fighting or those who had been wounded. Flag days, concerts, street collections and fairs certainly helped, but with more and more wounded arriving at the railway station, it was never going to be enough. In November the Northamptonshire District Nursing Association launched an appeal, beginning with a Need for Nurses week throughout the first week of the month. This was intended to highlight the shortages suffered by the nursing profession, not simply because not enough women joined, but because an awful lot who had were serving abroad, close to the front line. This meant less nursing available in the local hospitals and also less midwifery nursing accessible. What the association hoped to do was raise around £1,000 in extra revenue. As Earl Spencer put it:

> *In the circumstances created by the war – the wastage of human life on the battlefield, the lamentable infant mortality at home, the scarcity of doctors – the necessity for increased financial resources is urgent, and we are glad to give the people of Northamptonshire the opportunity of co-operating with us in such a cause.*

Essentially, what they were trying to do was set-up a district nursing centre that would house medical staff who could handle most medical needs, both from those who lived in the area and also the wounded that would inevitably be returning home, if their wounds prevented them from re-joining their regiment. Lieutenant Colonel Hitchens of the Royal Army Medical Corps, a man very well-known in Northampton, had already published a letter expressing his own concerns, which had been duly published and read widely:

> *Out here (writing from the front), we are concerned with the care of the sick and wounded in the army, and only see the first stages in what is often, I am afraid, the painful progress of the disabled soldier from the battlefield to his home. In many cases a complete cure is obtained, but there must always be a large residue of wounded who have finally to take their place at home.*
>
> *For many years to come our country will have to face as one of the aftermaths of the war, the problem of how best to help the brave lads and men permanently injured in her service. This help will have to be given in various ways and will be one of the greatest national duties we have to face.*
>
> *In a rural county like Northamptonshire with a large scattered population in villages and hamlets, there is bound to be a great number of disabled soldiers far from medical care that can be more easily given in a large town For them the District Nurse, co-operating with medical advice, will prove of invaluable assistance.*

The appeal met with huge success in the run-up to Christmas, as people recognised the need and began to grasp the point that this war was going to return more and more men with disabilities. They were already aware. They saw soldiers without limbs, men who were blind and men who were unable to walk, so people gave readily and the targets set were easily exceeded.

But there were also other things to cope with as December dawned. Food shortages had worsened. The *Mercury* published new food orders issued by the government, which were meant to control the use of flour, wheat and sugar:

BREAD – Millers are required to add to the percentage of 76 (%) now extracted from wheat a further percentage of not less than 5 (%) either by a further milling of wheat or by the addition of flour derived from barley, maize, rice, or oats.

WHEAT – The use of wheat for any purpose except that of seed or of making flour is prohibited

FEEDING OF GAME – The use of any grains required for food or feeding stuffs or for the purpose of food for game birds is prohibited

SUGAR AND CHOCOLATES – The manufacture of extravagant sweets is stopped. A maximum retail price of 3d an ounce for chocolate and 2d an ounce for other sweetmeats is fixed.

CAKES AND PASTRY – The use of sugar or chocolate for the external covering of cakes, pastry, or similar articles is prohibited.

They went on to inform the public that the price paid for potatoes, for retail in shops, would be fixed in 1917. All imports of oats from Ireland would be stopped, and police were to be given the powers necessary to allow them to enter any warehouse where food products were stored. As an addition to these restrictions in the food industry, coal would also be rationed. Amounts allowed per household would be dependent upon the number of rooms in the house. Things on the Home Front were getting a little more difficult.

Not helped either by arguments that had broken out in the boot and shoe industry between Northampton manufacturers and Kettering manufacturers. Kettering factory owners argued that their trade had slowly slipped away into Northampton throughout the year, brought about, they claimed, because more men from Kettering were conscripted than in the neighbouring town. Northampton manufacturers stood accused of appealing compulsory military service on behalf of every conscripted man in their factories on spurious grounds, thus delaying their enlistment, sometimes by months and supported in this endeavour by an appeals tribunal committee that was far more lenient in Northampton than elsewhere in the county. Northampton, of course, denied this and countered with their own loss of trade figures as they had been unable to supply the American market, which had offered them £1million of business but they had been unable to fulfil the order due to demands by the army. It was a spat that caused a degree of bad feeling between the two towns but essentially fizzled out as winter progressed.

Elsewhere the Rector of Bugbrooke found himself at the Northampton police court, charged with allowing the ringing of three church bells one hour after sunset. It contravened DORA, which prohibited any sound outside daylight hours that would be audible for any distance. Hostile aircraft used both sound and light to navigate to their targets. He was fined 4 shillings (20p).

Farmers breathed a sigh of relief when a wild cat, which had been responsible for the deaths of a huge number of ducks, fowls and hens,

Bugbrooke Church.

Christmas tree decorated with toys, mainly dolls.

was finally cornered and shot dead. Butter went up to one shilling and nine pence per pound (9p), eggs were selling at around 6d each (2½p) and the potato crop was reportedly low due to disease.

So, Christmas, like the one a year earlier, was understandably a quiet affair, marked more by Prime Minister Asquith's resignation and Lloyd George's rise to power, along with America's voice heard for the first time, as President Woodrow Wilson began to pressure Germany into looking for a peaceful solution to the conflict. Northampton's new mayor, John Woods, with his wife and daughter toured the almshouses on St Giles Street, where they distributed chocolate to the inmates. Then onto the orphanage for girls, where each girl was given a 3 penny piece, as were those at the Doctor Barnardo's home in Castilian Street.

At the Northampton army barracks, they distributed free cigarettes to the soldiers. Those at the Nazareth Home received chocolate and tobacco. Then, onto the Fever Hospital, Welford Road Hospital, Weston Favell Hospital and those at Duston, Dallington and Abington Avenue, where packs of cigarettes were issued to every wounded soldier. For them Christmas day particularly was exceptionally busy but no doubt rewarding. Certainly they were well-received and at the workhouse, where they ended the day, they were well-fed. On the Western Front, after the slaughter of the Somme, all was reasonably quiet as the year drew to a close.

CHAPTER 4

1917
The Town Digs In

January 1917 was a month of hard frosts. Across the town people struggled to heat their homes and feed their families. The war had reached stalemate again. There was a realisation that this was a war of attrition as much as it was military might. The countries more able to withstand the hardships and increase their industrial capacity were going to be the victors. But life for many had become extremely difficult. Submarine warfare, which had been steadily increasing in intensity, began to make a significant impact on our imports. Losses on the war front impacted on the labour market, despite the introduction of more women into the workforce. In turn, that meant we either had to grow more or ration what little there was.

The government had appointed Lord Devonport as minister of food. A man all too familiar with food and the retail trade, he issued a grave warning to all at the start of the year:

> *People who can afford a wide variety of food should eliminate bread entirely from lunch and dinner, and so preserve bread for people who must depend upon it. To ask an agricultural labourer to subsist on four pounds of bread a week would be a mockery; but to be safe, the average must be brought down to four pounds per head, and every*

German submarines caused havoc amongst shipping throughout the war years.

individual should try to reduce his consumption below that amount.

If they fail to do it, there will be compulsory rationing in bread and other foods.

When the members of Northamptonshire's Agricultural Committee met once again at the Grand Hotel, Northampton, it was this message that was on everyone's mind. A year ago they had met to discuss the ramifications of a war between armed forces. That same war was now a struggle between civilian populations. As farmers they were all too aware of what was needed, they had already met several times to debate the issues of shortages in agricultural labour. This time it was to discuss the use of additional land released to them under new legislation that had been passed in London. Large areas of land around Northampton previously closed to them had already been released for food crops. The recreation ground at Kingsthorpe was to be released to agriculture, Abington Park was to be given up for cattle grazing, as was a large portion of Victoria Park. At least 10 acres of land at Far Cotton was also to be returned to farming, along with a further 40 acres of land on the St Georges Avenue side of the racecourse, again for crop cultivation.

With the introduction of women onto the land having been agreed the previous year, farmers coped well working land currently in use. But expanding the acreage, as this new legislation demanded, meant

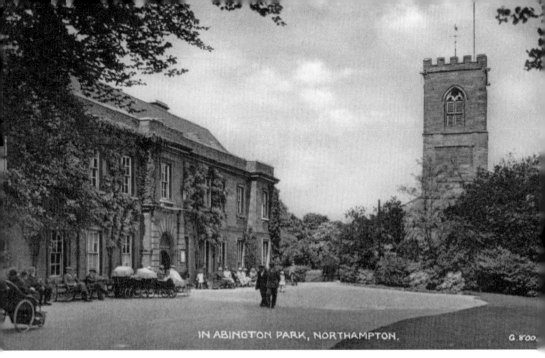

Abington Park.

the new labour force would become stretched and unable to cope. What they needed was an additional, probably temporary, labour resource. To that end it was decided, after lengthy discussion, to look for experienced farmhands amongst the German prisoners-of-war who were being held at the Eastcote Internment Camp. The government had already suggested the possibility of using captured soldiers, something that had been resisted, but with the worsening food situation opinions were forced to change. As a result, though with some reluctance, the army based in Northampton, after listening to the arguments put forward, agreed to release seventy-five German prisoners, under guard, to the Northampton farmers. A sound decision given the needs of both town and county.

Elsewhere, the call that had been made in 1916 to create allotments wherever and whenever possible was re-echoed, but now not just for vegetables. This time what was wanted was for people to keep rabbits, poultry and bees, as part of the government's overall increased production plans for the growing season. Across the town the proposals had already been widely accepted. Wasteland, as well as gardens, was dug up. Gardening committees were formed. Local newspapers ran weekly articles on how to grow, what to grow, and where to grow a whole variety of short-term crops. The need for potatoes was widely publicised, along with sage advice on the type and variety available to the home garden. By spring, Northampton and its people were well and truly a part of the war effort.

They were also on the receiving end of news of further heavy losses, this time in Palestine at the battles for Gaza. The war against Turkey had perhaps slipped into the background over the last few months, with more being reported from the near continent than the Middle East. But in April and through May the casualty lists began to reflect losses from the desert war, particularly in the attacks at Gaza. Strongly defended by men of the Turkish Army, in the space of three weeks the British fought two battles before the town finally fell on the second attempt, after three days of heavy fighting in mid-April. News was sketchy with a number of men from the 4th Battalion Northamptonshire Regiment reported either killed or missing. The following letter, published by the *Mercury* from Lieutenant Colonel John Brown, who commanded the battalion, was the first indication many families had of just what had happened out in the desert:

Distributing parcels to German prisoners-of-war.

We were in both of the actions near Gaza. The first time our work was not onerous. During the second battle we had to make a frontal attack over 3000 yards of ground swept by artillery and machine-gun fire. The battalion was splendid. Every officer and man went straight to the task: never a one flinched or showed the slightest hesitation. At night the General told me that no troops in the world could have behaved better: it made one a proud man to be commander of such heroes.

The Steelbacks got their name because they could stand hard knocks without flinching. Well on 19 April the Territorial Battalion earned its right to stand by its Regular Battalion, which it has looked up to, and still does, as its model.

Of the 21 officers who went into action only one came out unhurt: the only other officer at the end left with the battalion being myself who received a slight wound in the left arm.

What it did not do, of course, was mention the overall losses, which were high. There is no doubting the bravery but overall the letter is perhaps a little sketchy and devoid of too much detail. Certainly, the letter was something the newspaper would have been eager to publish, if for no other reason than its rallying call. For the families whose men had been a part of it, the casualty lists told a different story, particularly where the lists showed considerable numbers of men listed as simply missing. This was probably not lost on Colonel Brown, and later in the year the *Northampton Herald* published a second letter. This had been written some time after the battle and told how he had returned to the battlefield and how he and others had successfully identified some of the lost men:

We are resting on the cliffs a few miles north of Gaza ... Yesterday was the first day I was able to leave the regiment for a few hours, so the Padre, Doctor and I rode to the scene of the fight on April 19. It was a bad day, a ramseen was blowing and one could not see very far. A party of some 200 men from another division were clearing up the field, but still many bodies were lying just as they fell in April. Some were within a few yards of the Turks trenches, but they had made no effort to bury them.

We found about sixty of our men, and the officers found included Lieutenants Marlow, Lines, and Underwood. To all these we gave Christian burial on a hill which is officially known as Northampton Mound, for it was upon this very hill that our men made their gallant stand on that fateful day, and from which they prevented the Turk leaving his trenches for a counter attack. Lieutenant Marlow was lying with thirty-three of our men in a group between fifty and one hundred yards from the Turks front line ... other parties are searching the ground I hope to find traces of others ... The total casualties are stated to be about half the section of the battalion engaged.

Unusual to have allowed so much detail into the public arena but, for many at last, it began to fill in the blanks and from the late summer through to mid-winter more names were finally identified as either killed or prisoners-of-war.

On the Western Front, while news from the desert had been hitting the newspapers, a new British offensive was launched at Arras, with the 7th Battalion Northamptonshire Regiment, known by this time as the Mobbs Own Battalion, in action in support of the Canadians at a place named Vimy Ridge. It was heralded a success by British Commander Douglas Haig and reported in all local and national newspapers, with over 11,000 prisoners taken along with a number of guns. But, like all the previous battles, it eventually fizzled out into another stalemate, and war in the trenches continued as it had done for the previous three years. The only bright light on the horizon, so to speak, was that America had finally declared war on Germany, a decision brought about, in part, because of the submarine warfare.

Despite the American president's protests to Germany, her navy did not discriminate when it came to sinking merchant shipping, and the losses had finally become unacceptable to the United States. The Allies now had much needed help from across the Atlantic. The outlook was a little more optimistic.

Back home there were more mundane matters for people to deal with. Northampton's licensing trade held a meeting at the Town Hall to discuss the general state of business in the town, the upshot of which was that if profits were to recover, then the price of beer had to be increased. There was no opposition to the proposal of such an increase. The trade had been struggling for months, mainly due to production costs and the shortening of opening hours. With the new scale of charges agreed,

American President Woodrow Wilson.

it was hoped this measure would alleviate some of the pressure landlords and the industry generally had found itself under:

ALE	6d a pint
	3d a half pint
BOTTLED ALE	7d a pint
	4d a half pint
BOTTLED STOUT	9d a pint
	4½ d a half pint

Under the Defence of the Realm Act, pubs across Northampton had suffered in a variety of ways. When pub opening hours were reduced back in the summer of 1914, custom had obviously fallen away. Those still drinking discovered the strength of the beer had been lowered, and they were prohibited from buying a round of drinks. Profits inevitably fell as a result, as did overall levels of beer production. These effects were compounded further by the introduction of the Daylight Saving Act, which had effectively forced more people to remain indoors. There was probably little choice for the licensing trade if it wanted to remain in business. Rents and wages still had to be paid, and with margins squeezed ever tighter, there simply was no alternative.

Northampton Town and County Hall.

There was little resistance or argument from most people who, by this time, had become used to price increases. Most things on the domestic front were in short supply. For the army, who were not suffering from problems with food, and who tended to avoid alcohol consumption at the best of times, the key shortages were in livestock. Horses to be precise. For the previous three years they had been constant in their demand across town and county for animals capable of working in a variety of spheres on the battle-front. By late spring, with losses mounting, they were in desperate need of horses capable of pulling heavy artillery. The call had gone out for all businesses to bring their horses into Northampton's cattle market, where each animal would be assessed and judged as to its potential usefulness. One of the largest round-up of animals of the war began and resulted in over 600 horses being herded into the market for formal examination by the remount division of the army. For those owners who refused, or felt their animal not to be of the required standard, it meant they ran the risk of receiving a police visit. Most complied. Van horses, cobs, hunters, ponies, cab horses, and brewers' dray horses arrived throughout a single day, with each and every animal given a thorough check over. The net result was that only twenty-one animals fit the bill, for these the army paid a fair market price. The rest were returned.

The pressures of war were having an impact in virtually every walk of life. From shopping, clothing and food to leisure and sport, no household was ever really far away from the effects of war. By this stage of the conflict every household was caught up in virtually every aspect of the tragedy taking place across the Channel. Husbands, sons or brothers were either fighting or else working in industries that supported the war effort. Women were seconded into the labour force, occupying roles once solely the domain of men. Homes were requisitioned by the army to billet men in training. Gardens, open spaces, waste ground and public recreation areas were planted out to provide food. Even museums and art galleries were forced to end their evening openings and change their various exhibitions to better reflect the war effort. Churches were places of sanctuary and support as they dealt with the severe emotional stress felt by families in the communities they served. Engineering industries turned to munitions. The whole workforce of the town was forced to adapt and change as central government began to demand more and more productivity, and no one ever seemed to whinge. There was a let's-get-on-with-it attitude, this despite the unavoidable awfulness of war that they saw every day of their lives. Wounded men, amputees, grieving relatives and weekly reports of seemingly never-ending lists of casualties from the Front. Yet at no point were there riots, demonstrations or public denouncements of either Parliament or the army commanders in the field. War was simply an accepted fact of life, a burden to be borne, a war to be won.

Neither did there appear to be any animosity felt toward the growing number of prisoners-of-war housed at the Northamptonshire prisoners of war camp at Eastcote House. Leastways not publicly. Originally intended to house only civilians in 1914, two years later it generally housed those of German birth thought to pose a threat to security no matter how unreal. By 1917, that had changed significantly. Gone were the civilians to be replaced with military prisoners only, many of whom

The dining hall at Eastcote Prisoner-of-War Camp (Northampton Central Library).

at this stage of the war were employed around the county in varying forms of low key labour. Sometimes they also escaped.

Resourceful and determined, which was probably to be expected from men held in a military prison, they generally made a beeline for the coast for obvious reasons. In the spring of 1917, the local newspapers carried stories of one such escape by three prisoners. Dressed in civilian clothes, one with passable English language skills, they had simply disappeared. Police issued an alert and people were asked to be wary of strangers. Over a period of several days the search continued, with all three eventually captured as they walked along a road toward the coastal town of Southwold. It later transpired they had travelled from Northampton by train to Cambridge, where they bought food and goods from local shops, then travelled again by train to Ipswich and Halesworth, and finally on foot until stopped by a local beat bobby. Had it not been for one of the three telling the policeman that they were 'all Breetish', they probably would have got away with it. When questioned, they readily accepted that they were going nowhere and told police that they had intended to steal a fishing boat, hence the compass and German flag found in their possession. It appears that all escapees were caught and totalled eighteen in number during the length of the war.

By mid-summer, the fetes, fairs and garden shows that had become regular annual events were in full swing. The annual hospital parades had been, or were in the process of being, put together in both town and county. Northampton General Hospital, more than in any previous year, was in desperate need of more increased funding at this stage of 1917. At a meeting of the hospital governors held at the Town Hall, it was announced they had to raise another £10,000 to comply with the military requirement that they begin accepting soldiers whose wounds had healed and were being discharged from other hospitals, but whose injuries rendered them paraplegic. In past years these men had been sent back to their homes without any back-up care and, as their number had increased significantly, it had obviously become necessary for that to change. These soldiers needed a great deal of care and support that they could never receive in a home environment. That, claimed the governors, quite rightly meant that the hospital needed a refurbishment programme that would enable it to add the type of nursing required that would facilitate that kind of care. According to figures they published they would need a central heating system to create hot water on tap and steam for sterilisation. This would cost £6,000. In addition, they would need to provide a scientific research facility to help create the right sorts of medication. The building would need cleaning throughout and repainting where necessary. Monies raised by the various parades and celebrations were crucial to success, and the town reacted accordingly, as it had done throughout the war years, with many again giving generously to help attain the target they had set.

Sadly, as that meeting of governors came to a close, they received news that Edgar Mobbs had been killed in action. The England and Northants rugby player, who had almost single-handedly raised the 7th Battalion, was killed at Zillebeke during the Third Battle of Ypres, more often called Passchendaele. Lord Spencer addressed the meeting in order to break the news:

I was inexpressibly shocked this morning to hear that our gallant friend, Colonel Mobbs, had fallen in battle. We, who knew Colonel Mobbs, knew he was a most admirable organiser, a patriotic man, a born soldier. We regret his loss, but even in our regret we cannot help feeling most immensely proud of him and his battalion. If he could have chosen his mode of passing from this life, he would have chosen the mode in which he has left it, with his face to the foe surrounded by his own men. He has made a magnificent record for the 7th Battalion, of which we must forever be proud.

In the void that he has left for those belonging to him, no word we can speak can properly assuage their grief, but his name will be inscribed on the roll of honour amongst many others of his fellow countrymen in the Borough and County, and will be a beacon light to generations that come after. Colonel Mobbs, farewell to you, brave and gallant gentleman.

Wonderful words sincerely meant. Edgar Mobbs, DSO, died for a cause he believed in amongst men, who, in the main he knew and trusted. There was a sense of sadness across the town as the news spread.

After the meeting, at which Lord Spencer had spoken so eloquently, a memorial fund was set-up and raised £651 almost overnight. His name is still remembered, even today, and his statue can be found in Northampton's garden of remembrance. From 1921, to mark his importance to the town and to rugby, it was decided that Northampton Rugby Club would play what became known as the Edgar Mobbs memorial match each year. The match has endured and is still played today.

The memorial built to commemorate Edgar Mobbs.

The battle around Passchendaele raged for over three months. It is the one battle fought in the First World War that is remembered not just for the enormous loss of life, but also for the mud. It was a battle fought across a landscape devoid of trees. A morass of mud and water filled shell-holes where men would die, not just from bullets but from drowning. The land was essentially a bog and the weather throughout was absolutely frightful. Guns jammed, tanks sank into the mud, and thousands died either from the numerous German machine-gun posts that dominated the whole area or as a result of inhaling the lethal mustard gas that they used to halt the various advances. A place of devastation and death that did nothing to advance the Allied cause.

As news of this disaster filtered through there came news of another battle, this time fought on the Belgian coast. The Battle of the Dunes, as it became known, was a desperate fight that involved the Northamptonshire's fighting against overwhelming odds. Casualty lists, which had been steadily growing, reflected the fact that the fighting had been extremely heavy. Details at a local level were extremely sketchy and it was some time before the real story of just what had taken place hit the national press. When it did, people began to read of the Northamptonshires and the King's Royal Rifle Corps, caught by a surprise advance by the Germans near Nieuport, a coastal town at the end of the Allied line. Percival Phillips, of the *Daily Express*, wrote a week or so after the fighting:

> *Northampton men and their comrades of the King's Royal*
> *Rifle Corps bore the brunt of this German attack.*

According to his account this fierce, if under-reported, battle had cost dearly in terms of both lives and prisoners. The Northamptons had been ordered to fight to the last man, and essentially that's almost exactly what they did, many being killed either through shelling or the hand-to-hand fighting that followed as the Germans over-ran their positions. With nowhere to retreat, many were forced to surrender as their guns jammed, blocked by sand. For the families back in Northampton, there was no way of knowing who was a prisoner and who was not, a situation that endured until around mid-September, when postcards finally began arriving at homes across the town confirming prisoner status.

Many would never have read the description of battle outlined above, even more no doubt wondered how it was so many men died. Newspaper reports almost never talked of the losses, or used language the government deemed unpatriotic. War correspondents would never write articles that truly represented the war. If they had, these reports would never have seen the light of day. Soldiers were not allowed to take photographs. The only pictures that ever made it to the newspapers were of troop movements, group shots, the odd piece of ordnance, or the visiting hero. People tried to keep up-to-date by visiting the cinema. There, footage of troops moving up the line, horses moving artillery, staged action shots and so on at least gave the audience a sense of real involvement. But there was never any realism in what the public saw. No bodies, no images of a devastated landscape, the mud, the shellfire, the awfulness of trench warfare. None of that was allowed. So, throughout the war, those left at home were never made aware of exactly what was happening on the war front. They were only ever allowed to read stories of glory and derring do, and view sanitised images that were deemed patriotic or heroic.

By the fourth year of the war, the notion of trench warfare was almost a permanent fixture, and movement either forwards or backwards was commonplace and had a sense of constancy about it. News was what people craved. Everyone wanted to believe in success. Morale was still high but, from time to time, they needed to know that all the effort was not in vain. So, when local hero and well-known athlete Lieutenant George Reeve arrived at Northampton's railway station wearing the Military Cross, which had been added to his Military Medal, like William Boulter before him he was given a huge hero's welcome. A career soldier with twelve years' service, Lieutenant Reeve had fought at Mons, the Marne, the Aisne, the First Battle of Ypres, Second Battle of Ypres, the Somme, and Arras. Mentioned in despatches, wounded in the leg twice, wounded in the head and shell-shocked, he was more than deserving of his hero status. There can be no doubting George Reeve was an exceptionally brave man. Modest and unassuming, he told the gathering crowd that he only did his duty, and he earnestly believed that victory was in sight:

Though that road may be long and arduous, if we all keep our shoulder to the wheel I believe we would reach the victory and peace we all desire.

The crowd shouted and cheered then stood to sing the National Anthem before he was taken by coach through the town, cheered onward all the way to what was then the New Theatre, where a packed house waited to applaud him as he took his seat.

The fair, as advertised by the Northampton Mercury.

Patriotism was something keenly felt in Northampton, as the reception for Lieutenant Reeve clearly showed. People were keen to support the services that backed up the military, in particular the Red Cross. An appeal was made on their behalf back in the middle of the summer by their patron, Earl Spencer, as increased pressure on what resources they had meant that money was in constant short supply. What he proposed was a fundraising effort larger than any seen before. The sum needed was at least £15,000 if the Red Cross were to sustain the activities that had been so prevalent and successful over the previous three years. The intention was to run a series of events across the county throughout the summer months, culminating in a massive town fair and market to be held in Market Square. If all went to plan he and the Red Cross committee believed the sum could be achieved. What he asked for was commitment to the cause, and commitment was what he got. Parades, fetes, summer fairs, concerts, and street collections were carried out in virtually every town and village in the shire.

Red Cross ambulance 1917. (The Northampton Mercury)

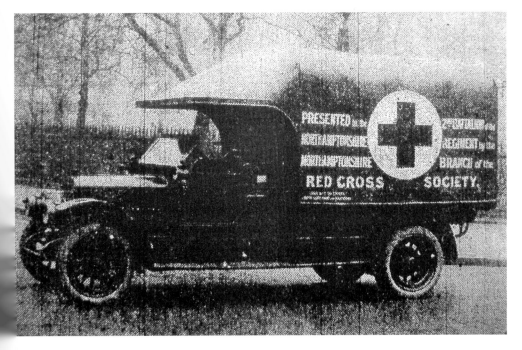

Businesses were canvassed to raise subscriptions, a weekly or monthly payment from those who could afford it to help ensure future funding, and people were asked to give their time freely in support of the soldiers in need of the type of care only the Red Cross could give. Response was huge. Not only from the public, but by a range of institutions they used. Churches and chapels raised weekly collections. All Northampton's theatres and picture palaces (cinemas) agreed to run at least one performance where all proceeds would be paid into the fund. Sport also joined in with the MCC agreeing to cricket matches being organised between Northampton and Bedford cricket clubs against Oundle schools, with all proceeds paid to the Red Cross. So by the time of the Northampton fair, over £7,500 had already either been raised or promised. Half the target was already in the bag before the biggest fair Northampton had ever seen opened at the end of September.

When the crowds arrived they found a market square that had been totally transformed. A huge replica of Northampton's old town gate had been built, complete with embattlements, turrets and arches through which everyone had to pass on arrival. The square itself was enclosed by a framework of canvas, with tall red Venetian masts placed at intervals and festooned in brightly coloured streamers. Within lay forty stalls, laid out in avenues, all decorated with flags, banners and bunting.

Every stallholder was dressed in different-coloured smocks or wearing white dresses with scarlet coloured aprons. The stalls sold a massively diverse number of products from army boots, ladies' fancy footwear, linen, paintings and fancy needlework to vegetables, fruit and flowers. Side shows had Punch and Judy for the children, boxing shows, piano recitals and even ventriloquists. Outside the square farmers ran a livestock sale and concerts were held in the evening. A massive and hugely successful event, the money raised far outstripped the £15,000 target, with expectations that by the end of the two-day event the fund would reach £20,000 with more, smaller events promised for autumn.

These built the fund even higher making sure, for 1917 at least, the Red Cross had sufficient funds to increase its activity throughout the winter and into early 1918. A resounding success all round, and no

The market square as it was during the Great War.

doubt much-needed and particularly praiseworthy when most families were facing real hardship as winter started. Coal had been in short supply throughout the year, and supplies worsened as the year drew to a close, with alternatives or useful additives being sought to help keep the home fires burning. The coal industry had been struggling throughout the year, forcing the government to take control. Labour shortages had put the pits in many areas on three-day-weeks and being compelled to supply coal in order that the country could maintain its armament industry added even more pressure. Therefore, the average Northampton household struggled to keep a fire in the grate throughout the coldest months of the year. Trying to obtain fuel oil as an alternative proved no more successful, with main supplies coming from America, and Germany's U-Boat campaign successfully sinking more and more merchant shipping, oil too was in short supply. The bulk of oil imports, of course, went direct to the Royal Navy, whose ships needed 12,500 tons of the stuff every week. So, for Northampton households, winter 1917 was extremely bleak. Many homes, already restricted on their fuel usage, were also struggling to feed their families more than once a day. Even the staple for most, potatoes, were hard to obtain and queues at grocery stores commonplace.

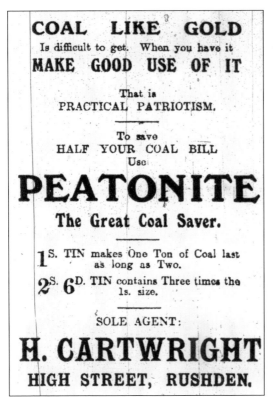

COAL LIKE GOLD

Is difficult to get. When you have it

MAKE GOOD USE OF IT

That is
PRACTICAL PATRIOTISM.

To save
HALF YOUR COAL BILL
Use

PEATONITE

The Great Coal Saver.

1S. TIN makes One Ton of Coal last
as long as Two.

2S. 6D. TIN contains Three times the
1s. size.

SOLE AGENT:

H. CARTWRIGHT

HIGH STREET, RUSHDEN.

Making coal last longer was a key requirement for most households.

The government restricted the price at which potatoes could be sold to no more than a penny a pound, to create a stable market. But even that was a difficult price to pay for some homes in the town when added to the rising cost of other foods. Poster campaigns were used to drive home the message that everyone had to use less, create no waste and cook wisely. Even campaigns advised households how to create fuel out of clay and sawdust. Things were tough for many but, despite all this, morale was still high.

At the Front, comforts for the troops continued to arrive, cigarettes perhaps the most important, even a necessity for most soldiers, as Private Williams from Northampton wrote:

> *Send some more smokes dad if you can, the more the merrier. Also need more socks if mum can manage it.*

The 'smokes' were sent along with a long list of other comforts, just as they had been in the previous years. As for socks, it was time to get the knitting needles going. Things like socks, scarves and mittens were in constant demand in the trenches as winter set in, and most families were more than adept at making them at home. Most women, at this time, were skilled in a range of home crafts. Needlework, knitting, rug-making and so on were commonplace skills learned when young were now meeting demand throughout the war years.

As a boost to Northampton's fund for comforts, but this time in aid of British prisoners-of-war, Northampton County Cricket ground played host to the first ever Mobbs memorial rugby match, attended by a huge paying crowd. Teams from South Africa and New Zealand turned out on a cold December day to play the first match of what would become an annual event – a much needed morale boost for the time.

Christmas, like years before, was another quiet affair. On the Western Front, British tanks attacked an unsuspecting German Army

Knitting for the soldiers was something heavily promoted throughout the war.

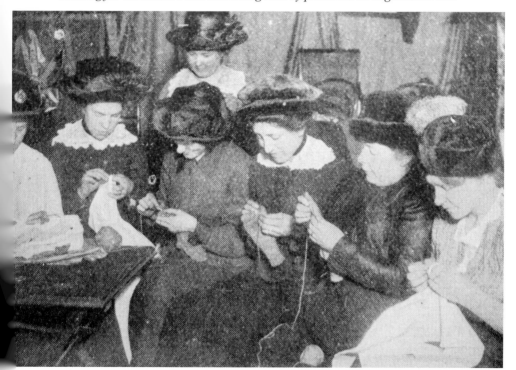

and achieved a resounding victory. Unfortunately, so successful, the generals failed to follow it up and, after ten days of fighting, everyone was back where they started. On the Eastern Front, the Russians revolted and effectively returned home. In the Middle East, Jerusalem surrendered to the Allies and American soldiers began arriving in France in significant numbers.

News also filtered through about a man who would become one of the greatest fighter aces of the First World War, Northamptonshire's Mick Mannock. Awarded the Military Cross back in the summer, his identity had remained hidden from a wider audience due to the restrictions placed on the press by the government not to reveal the names of pilots, unlike their counterparts in Germany, whose Aces went on to great fame and recognition. Here they were referred to as Captain X, something that would not change until January 1918, though obviously he was known locally. Mannock, Irish-born but living in Mill Road, Wellingborough, when war broke out would go on to be one of Britain's greatest fighter Aces.

CHAPTER 5

1918
The Final Act

December 1917 had proved to be the heaviest month on record in terms of the number of wounded received into Northampton's hospitals. In total, there had been nine train convoys of sick and wounded men brought into the town from overseas. Around 800 patients were brought straight from the Front, which meant that by the start of 1918 hospitals were at full capacity. At a meeting held in Northampton that January, the Red Cross reported they had treated in total some 1,800 men throughout the previous four or five weeks and had utilised every available bed. According to Earl Spencer, who chaired the meeting, the army had requested that they increase the number of available beds in all hospitals in order that they could meet the increasing demands made on them by the army's medical corps. But, owing to the difficulty experienced during the latter part of 1917 in procuring food and medical supplies, it was decided to refuse the request until the situation could be clarified. It was a valid and fair point. All the hospitals in Northampton had been working under considerable pressure for some time. Shortages in food and medicines, which had been building since the previous summer, added another burden to the already pressured medical staff. Added to these factors was the reduced number of nurses available to supply care. Bed numbers were not in themselves difficult to increase. The town had already converted the swimming baths at Barry Road into a ward by covering over the baths and bringing in fifty more beds, and could do more. In fact, total bed numbers by January 1918 that the Red Cross had access to was just over 1,200, which was a huge increase on what had been available at the start of the war. But unfortunately all were occupied. It was supplies that had become the greater concern, as it was for the rest of those living in the town.

Margarine and butter were virtually unobtainable and, in Kettering, margarine rationing had already been brought in. Meat supplies were also severely depleted, with Northampton operating at around twenty-five per cent of its needs. According to local butchers, they needed a weekly supply of ninety-four cattle and 460 sheep to maintain supply to the town's households. What they were receiving through the cattle market was around sixty cattle and only 180 sheep. Queues formed outside butchers' shops on a daily basis, which in turn forced the government to begin releasing quantities of frozen meat into the food chain. Generally of poor quality, this addition was nonetheless much-needed to plug the gap caused by the lack of supply from farms around the county. From the farmers' point of view, they had been suffering from huge shortages in animal feed and what they were able to source had been fed to their dairy herds. Milk for the family and growing children was seen as a priority, a policy agreed with the National Union of Farmers, whose instructions were to feed beef cattle only on root crops, grass and any fodder crops available, then release cattle to market in a lean state to try and maintain some supply. Once again U-Boat activity was having a detrimental impact on the home market.

In Germany, the situation was reported as even worse. Towards the end of January, amongst the wounded being ferried back from France was Northamptonshire flying officer, Lieutenant Henry Cooper, who had been shot down behind German lines and badly wounded. Captured and taken to a hospital in Mons, where he was treated for three bullet wounds in his back, he told Northamptonshire reporters that many operations there were carried out without the use of anaesthetic:

> *Five or six men would hold the victim's limbs, whilst, in full view of others waiting their turn, the surgeon performed his operation.*

Taken from Mons, he had travelled and stayed in Hanover, Karlsruhe and Treves, before being invalided back home, so had seen the situation in Germany at first-hand. According to his story, food was in very short supply across the whole country. Many subsisted on only black bread and acorn coffee, described by the lieutenant as an intensely bitter concoction, without sugar, which was extremely hard to obtain. Parcels from home, which had eventually found him, helped keep him alive. Clearly the war was having an equal if not worse effect on the German people than it was at home, despite the war at sea.

Nevertheless, peace was not yet in sight and the need for money to continue the fight was still a priority. To that end, Northampton organised Tank Week at the end of February. The idea behind it was to persuade people that putting their own money into War Bonds was a legitimate way of helping the war effort, at the same time offering no financial risk. These bonds had been in existence for a number of years but there had always been a little resistance to buying them, often due to a lack of understanding about how they worked coupled with the fact that money was always in short supply. The notion of bringing a tank to the town was obviously a good sales gimmick. This was new technology.

Probably one of the most decisive inventions of the war, it had a dual purpose throughout 1917 – 18, it was used to raise money and to win battles.

COPYRIGHT E.L.P.C?   ONE OF OUR TANKS   PASSED BY CENSOR

People had read about tanks and of their success on the war front, so to see one ought to bring in huge crowds, and it did. The tank arrived and spent a few days undergoing a mechanical check and had its paint touched up. It was then planned to be driven to the market square, where it would be parked up for a week. The *Northampton Mercury* published the route it was to take – Marefair, Horsemarket, Broad Street, Regent Street, Campbell Street, The Mounts, Abington Street and then finally into the square. On the due date, hundreds turned out to line the streets and welcome this dreadnought to the town. Flags waved, bands played and people cheered. Unfortunately, the technology was not good enough to guarantee the mechanics and it broke down before it covered half the route, something tanks of this period tended to do a lot. Despite their best efforts, the army were unable to rectify the problem. Disappointed crowds returned home and the tank, which had been given the name 'Ole Bill', was eventually transported to Market Square where it was parked up ready to do its bit in the coming sales week.

Support from all quarters ensured the tank was a massive success. Throughout its time in Northampton, thousands turned out to see it, touch it and revere it. Newspapers from all over the district, and outside the county, made great news of its stay and of the reason it was in town. War Bonds and War Savings Certificates, as the press constantly stressed, were a way to assist the men fighting the war:

> *Old Bill is a hungry customer. No matter how much you feed him he always wants more, for he has the appetites of a thousand Oliver Twists. If he was a meat eater there would be trouble.*

He certainly did have an appetite for money. The fundraising involved not just the public but also business institutions, retail shops, unions, various clubs, churches and sporting events. For those who felt they could not afford to hand over hard-earned savings, there were always insurance companies, some of whom would sell bonds on 5-, 7- or 10-year terms, thus everyone could become involved if they supported the cause. Thousands did, and by the time it left Northampton, the tank had raised the staggering sum of £1,609,951.

Within days of all this excitement came news of further casualties amongst the men serving in the Northamptonshire Regiment out in Palestine. After the battles around Gaza at the end of 1917, the war had moved on toward Jerusalem. Reports of those killed or wounded in battles fought to secure its capture began filtering through during February. Newspapers published a letter from an unnamed soldier, serving with the regiment, which helped give a little detail of what had happened out in the desert, though censors had removed his name and any of the various place names he had intended to reveal. The action he refers to took place at the end of November 1917:

> *There were three main attacks shortly after dawn, just before midday, and just after midday. We were in a tight corner. The day before Battalion Headquarters had moved into the local hotel. Colonel Brown, the Adjutant, myself, and two signal operators were sitting in the office when a high explosive shell hit the wall of the room ... You can imagine the dislocation, however we soon rigged up an office outside ... Then the shelling came on like rain. At the intensest part of the attack it was touch and go ... We knew the Colonel would never retire, and we were having heavy casualties. However, our fellows stood their ground splendidly and just as Battalion Headquarters was preparing for its last stand, the Turks slackened off pressure and retired.*

It made heroic reading and at least gave some information to families receiving telegrams about their loved ones on just what had been happening out there. Other sources of information were essentially none existent.

On 9 March, most of the troops stationed in Northampton marched from their barracks to the racecourse, where they paraded in front of hundreds of spectators. Crowds turned out not just to watch the soldiers but to witness the presentation of the Insignia of the Companionship of the Distinguished Service Order, posthumously awarded to Lieutenant-Colonel Edgar Mobbs and presented to his father, Oliver.

Brigadier-General Hill, who made the award, afterwards addressed the crowd:

> *The decoration awarded to Colonel Mobbs must appeal to you citizens of this town: he was one of you. He was a prominent figure in all that appertained to raising the physical standard of the manhood of this town and neighbourhood, and was one of those very rare personages, a born soldier. He was indeed a great personality – a man of great determination and imbued all ranks that had the honour to serve under him with that quality.*
>
> *In the dark days of 1914, when the call to arms came, he answered the call with alacrity, taking with him the flower of manhood of this neighbourhood. He had no previous military experience. He put his foot on the bottom rung of the ladder and by his innate genius for leadership his soldierly bearing, grit, and determination, rose in the short space of eighteen months to the command of a battalion, the officers and men of which were prepared to follow him to the gates of hell. He showed in his glorious death what manner of man he was.*

At the same ceremony, 10-year-old Peter Gunning also received a posthumous award of the Distinguished Service Order on behalf of his father, Brigadier-General Gunning.

By the end of the month the Germans had launched a major offensive along the Western Front, intended to bring the war to a conclusion before the Americans were in place to influence matters for the Allies. The attack, launched on the Somme, was initially a success, the British being forced back 40 miles. Losses were heavy and reflected in the lists that began to appear throughout April. Though news at home was still scarce and the true events taking place under-reported, it was clearly evident, simply by the sudden increase in casualties, that something major had taken place. But like all previous attempts to bring the war to a conclusion, it failed. By April 1918, the long awaited

The memorial at Sixfields to Walter Tull.

American forces finally moved into the front line and the German advance stalled. An all too familiar stalemate ensued, though this time it would not last long.

Amongst those killed during this offensive was the Northampton Town inside forward, Walter Tull. Promoted in May 1917 to Second Lieutenant, he had been the first ever mixed-race combat officer in the British Army, enlisting at the outbreak of hostilities. After almost four long years fighting in Italy and on the Western Front, he was killed at the small village of Favreuil, in the Pas De Calais, on 25 March 1918. Experienced and brave, he had fought his way through the battles of Ancre, Somme, Messines, Ypres, Menin Road Bridge and Bapaume. He was recommended for the Military Cross but never awarded it, but is remembered today in the small garden of remembrance at the Sixfields Football Stadium. Sadly, though not known at the time, there is no grave as his body was never recovered.

News of his death, of course, did not break back in Northampton until several weeks later, by which time for many there were more pressing matters to concern them. Food rationing had been brought in during April to combat the acute shortages and distribution problems for meat, butter, sugar and margarine, forcing people in the town to register themselves with local retailers before they could receive their share of the meagre supplies on offer. Hoarding became a criminal offence, with fines imposed of between £2 and £10 per item. Discontent spread as queues lengthened and deficiencies became ever more prevalent. In Kettering, there had already been street protests when between sixty and seventy iron-stone workers had gathered in the town to voice their opposition to rationing and what they saw as the inequality of food distribution, claiming that their families were starving while those of more affluent means were not:

> *We must have some meat if we are to keep at our work. If we don't provide the iron how are they going to make the shells for fighting? … I went to any number of shops the other day and couldn't get even a bit of cheese or bacon.*

Elsewhere, queues had lengthened day-on-day as women waited for hours, in all weathers, in their attempts to buy food. With meat supplies still at critical levels, a meeting of local butchers took place at the Stag's Head in Northampton to debate the idea put forward by the government to form a butchers' wholesale association. The principle behind this was that all meat supplies would be handled and controlled by a single organisation that would buy the animals at market, slaughter them, then distribute the meat equally and fairly amongst the number of retail outlets across the town and surrounding areas, with each butcher paying cash to buy the supplies needed for their business to satisfy their own customer needs. The plan clearly had merit. It was accepted there would still be shortages, but competition for supply would be removed. The proposal made sense and after taking a vote it was readily agreed. To help alleviate the pressures that had dogged the farming industry throughout the war, the Women's Land Army was finally formed. A march through Northampton of uniformed women to advertise the

Lilford Hall, used by the army for wounded soldiers.

formation of this crucial organisation had gone some way to break down taboos and dismantle any prejudice the farming industry still harboured. Women were not to be seen as part-time workers in skirts playing with a hoe. Training in milking, horse work, mechanics and animal husbandry were carried out at a number of centres around the county, including Burghley House, Polebrooke, Lilford and, of course, the Experimental Farm at Moulton, which had been the first.

They had also been brought in to replace men in market gardening, forestry and osier work (willow canes used in basket-making), At last the xenophobia of earlier years had finally been overcome. There was even a new monthly magazine, the *Landswoman*, dealing with matters of interest to women working on the land, which added further esteem to the role if it were still needed.

While shortages did exist and were causing some stress to everyday lives, there was also a sense that things were changing. Families were coping and adapting to different ways of living their lives. All industries were at full capacity and household incomes were maintained at liveable levels, while news coming out of Germany and reported in both local and national newspapers was not so positive. There, strikes in key industries, protests against the war and general industrial unrest along with severe food shortages were causing a level of dissension

The Women's Land Army came into being in 1917 and solved the problem of managing the land effectively.

not seen before. So, in Northampton, there was more of an air of optimism about the town, something that had not been prevalent so much during the last few months. Victory was perhaps at last in sight, though, obviously, not imminent.

Since the German advance in March and the ensuing deadlock that followed, the Western Front had been quiet. Casualty lists returned to normal, that is reported losses had fallen from the high numbers reported back in spring. Less merchant shipping was also reported lost by U-Boat action. The navy had introduced the convoy system to combat German submarines with unprecedented success. They had also mined the sea between Orkney and Norway, which had prevented the U-Boats escaping back to their home ports. But the submarine war had not been completely eradicated, as a letter from an unnamed Northampton sailor testified:

> *The ship was torpedoed about a dozen or fourteen miles out, and I was thrown into the water. I was rescued by a second ship. There would not have been such a lot drowned if the U-Boat had not torpedoed our rescue ship after she was absolutely packed with injured and exhausted men ... I think I had about one hours swimming about altogether and when I was picked up I had managed to cover myself from head to foot with black, evil smelling oil from the tanks of the sunken boat ... many poor fellows were either sucked down by the boat and drowned before they came up, or else were badly injured by one of the two explosions ... I should not like to go through it again.*

The names of the two ships were censored, as was the sailor's identity, but thankfully he survived.

As summer progressed, this type of attack began to recede, which in turn meant more imports began to get through, though little was made of it in the local newspapers. Northampton had other things to worry about in the summer of 1918. The first cases of Spanish Flu were reported by the end of June, the start of what would become a world-wide pandemic, which would eventually kill more people across the world than died in the war. Generally a three-day infection and known in the trenches as 'La Grippe', it came to town in three waves. The first between June and August, the second and far more virulent in autumn, and the final stage over winter and into 1919. Headmistress of Northampton's St Andrew's Infant School, a Mrs Galsworthy, was amongst the first fatalities. Others followed particularly amongst the wounded. Spreading quickly as transference from one worker to another was so easy, it soon began to impact on industry at all levels. Trams had to cut their services, as did the railways. Northampton hospitals closed their doors to visitors, most schools were shut down and all cinemas and theatres advised to close while infection was at its highest. The sections of the populace hardest hit were those aged between 5 and 35, and the very old. By autumn, Kingsthorpe Army Camp was reporting numerous deaths amongst the soldiers and the town's medical authority was stretched almost beyond capacity, with over 4,000 schoolchildren infected. Overall it lasted for around eighteen months, and went away almost as quickly as it had arrived. Today, we still have no real idea of just how the disease mutated or whether it will ever return.

At the height of the pandemic, and perhaps somewhat overlooked because of it, news broke of the death of Northamptonshire's flying Ace Edward Mannock. Irish-born but living in the county at Wellingborough before the outbreak of war, he had worked for the town's National Telephone Company and had been secretary to the Independent Labour Party before enlisting. He was sent to Turkey in 1914, where he had worked as a telephone engineer, was interned and eventually returned to Northamptonshire in poor health in 1915.

He joined the Royal Army Medical Corps after he had recovered and, in August 1916, transferred into the Royal Flying Corps. After initially finding it difficult to fit in to the officer class he was serving with, he went on to become one of the greatest ever fighter Aces of

Edward Mannock, air Ace.
(Northampton Central Library)

the Great War. Officially credited with sixty-one victories at the time of his death (though some believe it was higher), he was also awarded the Military Cross and Bar, Distinguished Service Order and two Bars, and was later posthumously awarded the Victoria Cross. He was an exceptionally brave man, though his exploits were rarely reported due to the level of censorship in place throughout most of the war. Unfortunately, like Walter Tull, there is also no known grave.

Sadly, his would not be one of the last deaths reported in the casualty lists. By late summer 1918, the war still had some way to go before the horror would end. Raising money was still one of the main objectives of the town. Summer fetes and fairs continued to be the favoured method of raising money locally. All always well-supported by Northampton's hard-pressed population, most of whom were still cheerful, optimistic and deeply patriotic, buoyed by a positive press, both local and national, who continued to reassure them that the war was nearing its end, and that Britain would ultimately prevail. There were stories from the Front, the odd letter, photographs of those killed or wounded, and as the year progressed there was more and more about Germany's struggles at home.

Not that the newspapers were not having their own difficulties. Paper supplies had been seriously affected by the war, rising costs forcing them to reduce their size. In some parts of the country there had also been calls for the public to save paper that could be recycled, so desperate was the situation becoming for some. Yet despite the problems they continued to print and to report, whether it be good news or bad, and people continued to buy.

Desperate for news, and so far away from the war, newspapers were their only real source of information. Unlike today when we have access to news from around the world twenty-four hours a day, they had limited access. Nor were they able to read discerning, veracious accounts of the war due to the censorship prevalent at the time. Nevertheless, no matter how tenuous, it was a link to the men fighting at the Front, and through the casualty lists a reminder of the price being paid to bring the fighting to an end.

Not that people were unable to relax and enjoy themselves. The various summer events were an obvious release for many, a time to be out and about, despite the flu, meet others, be part of the numerous social events that tended to occupy the summer months. Theatres and cinemas, once the influenza infection had begun to die down, were also back in high demand, the cinema as much for the newsreels as for the

These type of postcards were in common usage through the war

entertainment, and the theatre for pure escapism. The wounded were also a key part of the town's activities with concert parties being a regular occurrence throughout the year. People enjoyed what they could of the longer days, many joined groups like the ladies' swimming club, or one of the various gardening clubs that had sprung up. There were lectures, talks, discussion groups and volunteer services to get involved with, not to mention numerous church activities, most of which were well-supported. After four years of war, routines were established with settled working hours the norm. Schools had managed, by and large, to stay in operation mainly through the employment of older or previously retired teachers replacing those who had gone off to fight. Habits, of course, had changed as would have been expected but by 1918 there was a sense of normality, albeit forced if not somewhat fallacious, but understandable.

Northampton Town and County Hall.

The same could also be said of the trench war. Since the failure of the German offensive earlier in the year and the stalemate that followed, a period of quiet inactivity seemed to have settled over the whole front line. The American forces, by this time well and truly embedded into the Allied lines, were now ready to be launched at the waiting Germans. Speculation was rife, both at home and in France, that another major offensive was about to be launched. When it came, in July, after much planning, it proved decisive. Lessons had clearly been learned from four years of war and, unlike all previous attempts to break the German lines, this time the generals got it right. By autumn the Allied army had smashed its way not just through the German trench system but also through the fortifications of the Hindenburg line. Reports coming back through the various newspapers began to talk of a war of movement not the trench warfare that had dominated war news since 1914. Suddenly, newspapers were full of successes on all fronts. People were reading of the collapse of Bulgaria, British advances in Palestine, the retreating armies of the Austro-Hungarian Empire, and the German army in retreat on all fronts. The war was in its final stages.

On 7 November, false rumour led to many in Northampton believing that an armistice had been signed. People spilled out onto the streets wanting to believe the war had ended only to be disappointed. But the end was very near. News finally reached the town by lunchtime

British soldiers following a tank during the 1918 offensive.

four days later. By one o'clock in the afternoon, the streets were thronged with people cheering, waving flags, hanging out bunting. Virtually every window in town was flying a flag, either the Union Jack or the Stars and Stripes. All industry was brought to a halt. No one asked to leave the factory or the shop, they simply went, desperate to join in the celebrations that went on throughout the rest of the day and through the long night. Churches rang their bells across the county, the lighting restrictions ended with immediate effect. Every church was full to capacity as people gathered to sing, cheer, pray and offer up thanks to God. Buttonholes worn at the various summer celebrations were brought out for the final time, the National Anthem was sung in the streets, cars hooted, trams emptied and everywhere became a riot of colour.

The war to end all wars was finally over.

Epilogue

Christmas 1918 was, perhaps surprisingly, a quiet, sober affair. The churches were well-supported on Christmas morning and most people spent the remainder of the day in their own family circle. Without doubt it was the first time in five years it was possible to celebrate the occasion and know with certainty that it truly was the Festival of Peace. Despite food restrictions, most enjoyed a day of plenty. The hospitals, workhouse and all charitable organisations ensured Christmas dinner was worthy of the day.

As had become the norm over the previous years, concerts, whist drives and all round entertainment had been put in place for the wounded. The Allied War Fund provided the usual gifts for those still recovering from wounds, and all retail shops remained closed for an extra day. There was an air of optimism about the town. This was the first occasion since the outbreak of war that people had felt able to relax and enjoy the celebration without any sense of pain, anxiety or guilt. Yet everyone was all too aware of the cost they had paid for the victory, both in the lives that had been lost and in the lives that been irrevocably changed, and that, no doubt, subdued the celebratory mood.

This was understandable as casualties continued to arrive in Northampton throughout November and December 1918. Many were severely wounded and most families still had husbands, sons or brothers out in France. Demobilisation was proving to be a slow process. Those who had jobs awaiting them seemed to be amongst the first to return. For thousands of others it was 1919 before they were repatriated to Northampton. Preference, of course, was given to soldiers who had been held as prisoners-of-war in German camps. For many the war had been a thoroughly miserable experience, often captured

The war is over, soldiers relax after the armistice had been signed.

after being wounded and then having to endure poor living conditions and exist on a limited, often restricted, diet. As news about the circumstances of their incarceration started to be reported, people were rightly angry at the treatment they had received, but also pleased as they discovered that their fundraising efforts had probably kept them alive. Such was the case of Private Payne, from Cedar Road in Northampton, whose story was published by the local newspapers:

All the time the German food supply was execrable, and hungry as we generally were, we could not tackle the stuff they put before us; but from February 1915, to December 1917, I was fortunate enough to get a supply of parcels sent out ... and ripping parcels they were too. The contents included tea, sugar, tinned meat, cocoa, and there were also packs of playing cards which came in very useful ... We cannot feel too grateful to those at home who showed their sympathy with us in such a practical manner. If it had not been for the parcels we received from the friends at home many of us would not have seen old England again.

For Private Payne the return home was obviously an intense experience. After over four years locked behind barbed wire, no doubt he experienced mixed emotions and a degree of apprehension as he got to grips with life once more as a civilian, particularly when it came to being re-employed.

Life in Northampton after the war changed forever. Women had occupied the roles men had left behind. Now, as the men returned from the war, many of these women were losing their place within the workforce. But they had got used to working during the war, had gained

Business began to return to normal as the war ended.

The War Memorial to the Dead of the World War in Northampton.

new skills, taken jobs in industries they would previously never have considered suitable, worked on the land, in transport and entered the medical profession. They had also won the vote, at least if they were over the age of 30. Still, it was a start and they were not about to give up their hard-won recognition. Besides, in many households there was no other breadwinner. Neither was there any future husband, the traditional prospect of marriage had ended with the war. Too many young men had been killed. In the Northamptonshire Regiment alone almost 6,000 men had died in the fighting. The role of women had changed forever.

So too had the long-held view that it was the upper classes who had the divine right to rule. The Labour Party was on the rise and would become unstoppable. Trade unions had blossomed throughout the war and at its end were growing in influence and strength. Churches began

The memorial to Walter Tull at Sixfields, near to the football stadium.

to see their influence wane, Victorian values were cast aside, and the type of work both men and women were prepared to take on had changed. The big houses and the role of their domestics in running them was also a part of this change. People no longer wanted to be a part of the serving classes as they had before the war. Politics began to play a greater role in people's lives and change was being demanded. Above all women had perhaps realised that the suffragettes had failed to bring the independence they sought, but the war had provided it through the notion that they could profit from the work they did, and that was not something they were going to give up lightly, and rightly so.

Not that any of this impacted immediately. All things take time and in Northampton at the start of 1919 unemployment was rife. Industries had lost the government contracts that had carried them through the war. For the shoe industry that had lost 2,574 men killed in action, it meant less work, which in turn reduced the numbers required to keep the industry moving forward.

Similarly, engineering no longer had work in munitions or vehicle manufacture, there had been very little house building, and so it went on across the whole of the town's industrial landscape. Men returning to a civilian life found life, at times, hard. But Northampton was a resilient town and over the following years it recovered from the war and all its problems. Employment returned, industries held on to their profits and invested, houses were built and confidence returned. The sad thing is that the war, with all the misery it brought, failed to resolve European tensions or quash German territorial ambitions, the consequence of which was the rise of the odious Adolf Hitler, a resurgent Germany and the heinous Nazi party.

Index